McLevy: The Edinburgh Detective

Such as met 'Jamie' for the first time might have taken him for a well-to-do farmer from the Emerald Isle on a visit to Scotland intent on a 'deal'. He was of medium height, square-faced, and clean-shaven, and always wore a tall silk hat, from beneath the broad brim of which a pair of quick black eyes scrutinised the crowd as he sauntered along the streets accompanied by his faithful companion Mulholland.

Edinburgh Evening News, *1922*

McLevy

❖

The Edinburgh Detective

MERCAT PRESS
EDINBURGH
www.mercatpress.com

First published in 2001 by Mercat Press
James Thin, 53 South Bridge, Edinburgh EH1 1YS
www.mercatpress.com
Stories first published in 1861 in *Curiosities of Crime in Edinburgh* and
The Sliding Scale of Life

Foreword © Quintin Jardine, 2001

ISBN 184183 0313

*The publishers would like to express their thanks to
Quintin Jardine and Rob Stainsby.*

Set in Bodoni at Mercat Press
Printed and bound in Great Britain by
Cox & Wyman Ltd

Contents

Foreword by Quintin Jardine	*vii*
Memoir of Mr James M'Levy	*xi*
The Blue-Bells of Scotland	1
The Broker's Secret	12
The Dead Child's Leg	20
A Want Spoils Perfection	31
The Breathing	41
The Child-Strippers	45
The White Coffin	52
The Cobbler's Knife	61
The Cock and Trumpet	72
The Widow's Last Shilling	81
The Happy Land	89
The Wrong Shop	95
The Letter	103
The Monkey-Jacket	112
The Coal-Bunker	125

The Mustard-Blister   137

The Pleasure Party   147

The Tobacco-Glutton   155

The Whiskers   162

The Club Newspaper   171

The Laugh   180

Foreword by Quintin Jardine

❖

It would be nice to say that James McLevy, for all that he was a man of flesh and blood, and that his stories are based on his own career, is the progenitor of all of the fictional Edinburgh detective policemen who have followed in his wake, up to and including today's anti-heroic figures, Ian Rankin's celebrated John Rebus, and my own dark character, Bob Skinner.

It would be nice to say that, but in my case, at least, it wouldn't be true. The fact is, I had never heard of McLevy until I was asked by Seán Costello if I would read some of his stories, and then consider writing a foreword to this republished edition of his work. I undertook to do the first part at least, then at once withdrew for a while into my own fictional world, leaving the pile of photocopies form Mercat Press gathering a fine layer of dust on my desk.

When finally I had sent *Head Shot* on down the road to London, ultimately into the hands of one of those people called copy editors—whose mission in life seems to be to boldly pick nits where no person has picked nits before—I blew it away and picked them up, expecting to find some pretty dusty prose inside. Wrong. Within five minutes I knew I was going to write the foreword; now that I'm doing it I regard it as an honour to have been asked.

McLevy writes of another time, another historical era. His characters and contemporaries are not people we know; they didn't even live in the tales we were told by our grandparents. Yet paradoxically, it is our world of which he writes. He walked many of the same streets we walk, and the crimes which he records in his stories are not far different from those of which we may read daily in the *Evening News*, or even in the *Scotsman*, another living link to McLevy's days.

Of course, narrative styles have moved on since he sat down to write these stories in the middle of the century before last; his is very much of that period and God alone knows what my copy editors would make of him. But the quality of the printed word is not eroded by time, and McLevy's tales more than pass the first and most important test, in that they remain an outstandingly good read, as well as being a very important contribution to the social history of that time.

They indicate too that political correctness was something of an alien concept in McLevy's day. He was an Irishman, come to seek work in Scotland, and his dislike of the English is nowhere hidden or understated. He cast a critical eye over the press of the day too, and the combination of his twin dislikes is beautifully expressed in the opening page of "The Pleasure Party", in which his natural talent as a writer is seen at its sharpest.

Yet most of all these stories are true crime classics, imbued with all the pathos, darkness and occasional humour that you will find in the best crime fiction. Take "The Cobbler's Knife" as an example; McLevy's account of the killing of one friend by another, and the bizarre circumstance that led up to it has an undertone of horror worthy of Poe. On the other hand, "The Pleasure Party", his tale of the apprehension of a quartet of hapless pick-pockets from England, up for the gullible and supposedly easy marks along Princes Street, is a comic gem, rounded off by the priceless sentencing speech of Sheriff Hallard, which seems to my layman's eye to contain grounds for appeal in every line.

There are timeless moments too. In "The Breathing", McLevy, in thoughtful pursuit of two robbers—muggers, in modern-speak— says to a constable, "Then stand you there, as steady as a post, but not as deaf. Keep your feet steady and your ears open." If I gave that line to Bob Skinner, the order would be exactly the same, if a little more terse, and perhaps with the odd adjective.

The seeds of the fictional anti-hero lie within the real-life character of McLevy. There is a clear impression of kinship in spirit between him and the people he pursues, and invariably apprehends; indeed, he knows most of them by name. This is not to say that he was a thief sent to catch another; far from it, the man is a moral paragon from the soles of his boots upwards. But he is of their stock, of their community, and he understands them and has more sympathy for them than is likely to be found towards their clients in most of today's inner city police forces—always acknowledging that their working environment is vastly different from the days of McLevy's perambulations around the Old and New Towns. (Clearly this is true in physical as well as social terms. For example, the two failed robbers mentioned earlier were spotted heading for "the valley between the Pleasance and Arthur Seat", a popular hideout of that time.)

The man was no soft touch; a reputation for heavy-handedness comes through on occasion. Yet he pursues his quarry, in most of his stories, more in sorrow than in anger. His sympathy for the unfortunate William Wright in "The Cobbler's Knife", as well as for his victim, is real and clear, and when, unexpectedly, the jury chooses to convict him of culpable homicide rather than send him to the gallows, the relief of the matter-of-fact McLevy is palpable. Yes, he knew wickedness when he saw it, but clearly in his life this was far from a common occurrence.

So how does James McLevy relate to my generation of fiction writers? How would Bob Skinner handle him if he were transported through 150 years or so? Very carefully, I should imagine; McLevy was clearly a one-off, a character who would have trouble fitting into a modern police force, yet whose perception and knowledge of his streets and his subjects would have made him too valuable to be excluded from it.

But the fact is, when I try to consider his work in the context of crime fiction as it has developed since his day, leading as it did to the emergence of Conan Doyle, I find myself thinking not of Edinburgh at all, but of somewhere long ago and far away. When I look through my limited encyclopaedia of fictional detectives and try to find a match for McLevy's street savvy and direct action, there are two who stand comparison best of all. Chester Himes, in the earlier books in the Harlem cycle, comes right at the top of my all-time-greats list. His characters, the jovially ferocious Coffin Ed Johnson and Gravedigger Jones have the same feel about them, for me, as the real-life James McLevy. And in his prose, in the humanity and humour with which he tells his stories, in his way of chronicling a unique era in the history of a unique city, the Victorian detective stands alongside their creator.

Memoir of Mr James M'Levy

From *Curiosities of Crime in Edinburgh*, 1861

❖

Mr M'Levy was born in the parish of Ballymacnab, county Armagh, in Ireland, his father holding the position of a small farmer. Having received a suitable education, at the age of thirteen he was apprenticed to the trade of fine-linen weaving, at which he continued till he was seventeen, when he came over to Scotland. Having remained for two years at the Gatehouse of Fleet, he came to Edinburgh, where he was first employed by Mr Wallace, a considerable builder at that time, and subsequently by Mr Walker, a son-in-law of Mr Wallace's. Latterly, he went into the service of Robert Paterson, builder and tax-surveyor. During all this time he conducted himself with honesty and propriety, occasionally displaying freaks of humour, and instances of that ingenuity which so signally marked his subsequent career.

In particular, Mr M'Levy had so recommended himself by his uniform steadiness to Mr Paterson, that that gentleman, who probably saw other qualities in him capable of being turned to better account than in the daily toil of a hod-man, advised him to enter the police, and promised to get Captain Stewart to accept his services. He immediately agreed to this proposal, and Mr Paterson having succeeded in his application, he entered the force in August 1830, as a night-watchman. In this capacity he acted till 1833, when, having taken fever, he was removed to the Infirmary. Though at one time dangerously ill, it was not long till, through the means of a strong constitution, he began to show symptoms of amendment; and at this stage there occurred an incident worth recording, as showing his turn for "finding people out." It seems the doctor who attended his ward, having noticed with satisfaction the returning convalescence of his patient, in whom he felt perhaps more than the usual interest, ordered nourishing food and wine for him. On the first day after this order, the nurse brought the supply. There was no objection to the food, but the patient thought the quantity of wine not only below what he wished and required, but so limited as to do him no good. He at once suspected the nurse of defrauding him of what he so much required. Accordingly, when the doctor came round next day and asked his patient how the wine agreed with him,—"Why, sir," said he, "it could not disagree with me, for I scarcely knew it was in my inside, it was so small." "Well, you shall have more," replied he; "I will give directions to the nurse." Next day the nurse appeared again, this time with a good quantity in a bottle. As she entered, M'Levy turned his eye, saw the bottle, and then throwing the clothes over his head, with room only for the play of one eye, began to snore loudly. Up comes the nurse, and being satisfied that her patient was sleeping, she put the bottle to her head, and took off nearly the half. "So, so," said the patient quietly, getting his head out, "this is the way my wine goes. Madam, this will be the dearest gulp you ever had in your life." Then the woman began to preach and pray, and appeal to his feelings,—that she would be turned away if he informed on her, and would, in short, be a ruined woman. But M'Levy would not say he would not inform—he kept his intention to himself, and the consequence resulted very happily for him, and not unhappily for the woman, who, from that day, gave him even more wine, not only raw, but in the form of negus, than he could swallow—all which tended to his convalescence.

After recovering from this illness, he was told by the doctor that he must renounce his night-work, and he accordingly went to Captain Stewart with the view of resigning. That gentleman, who had a quick eye to intelligence, and knew where to look for it, offered M'Levy promotion to the staff of detectives. He was accordingly appointed, in 1833, to that situation he has filled since with so much honour to himself and advantage to the public. His name soon came to be known everywhere, and for a thief or robber to be ferreted out or pursued by M'Levy, was held equal to his being caught. We have only to look to the number of his cases, 2220, to form some idea of the vast amount of property he has been the means of restoring to its owners, of the number of offenders he has brought to justice, and of the impression of his influence in the observed diminution of crime. Other causes, have, happily, tended to this last result; but it cannot be denied that, in so far as regards Edinburgh, much of that effect has been due to his exertions.

The
Blue-
Bells
of
Scotland

❖

There are apparently two reasons that influence some of our Edinburgh gentry in locking up their houses and ticketing a window with directions about keys when they go to the country. The first is, that they save the wages of a woman to take charge of the house; and the second, that they may tell their less lucky neighbours that they are able to go to the country and enjoy themselves. No doubt they trust to the watchfulness of a policeman, forgetting that the man has no more than two eyes and two legs, with too often a small portion of brains, which he uses in silent meditation—a kind of "night thoughts", not always about housebreakers and thieves. I have heard of some of the latter making fun out of these inviting locked-up mansions. "Bill, there's a ticket in the window about keys, but it's too far off to be read, and besides, you know, *we can't read.*" "No, and so we'll use a key of our own; we can't help them things."

I don't suppose that Mr Jackson, of Coates Crescent, entertained any such notions when, in June 1843, he locked up his house on the occasion of a short absence of some five or six days; but certain it is, that when he returned he found all outside precisely as he had left it—blinds down, shutters close, doors locked. All right, he thought, as he applied the key and opened the door; but this confidence lasted no longer than a few minutes, when he discovered that his top-coats which hung in the lobby were gone. Now alarmed,

1

he hurried through the house, and wherever he went he found al-most every lock of press, cabinet, and drawer, either picked by skeleton keys or wrenched off, wood and all—the splinters of the torn mahogany lying on the carpets. All right! yes, outside. If he had been cool enough he might have thought of the good man's cheese of three stones, laid upon the shelf for the christening, and when taken down (all right outside) weighed only the avoirdupois of the skin, the inside having been enjoyed by artists scarcely more velvet-footed; and yet the parallel would not have been true, for the thieves here had been most fastidious gentry—even refined, for, in place of carrying off most valuable articles of furniture, they had been contented with only the fine bits of jewellery, gold, and precious stones, such as they could easily carry away, and easily dispose of.

Finding his elegant lockfast pieces of furniture thus torn up, Mr Jackson had no patience to make inquiry into the extent of the depredations before coming to the Office and reporting the state in which he had found his house. When I saw him he was wroth, not so much at what might turn out to have been stolen as at the reck-less destruction; but the truth was, as I told him, that there was no *unnecessary* breakage. The thieves behoved to steal, and they behoved to get at what they wanted to steal. Few people understand the regular housebreaker. In almost all cases the clay is moulded, in infancy, moistened with the sap of stolen candy or fruit, and the glare of angry eyes only tends to harden it. We always forget that the thief-shape is the *natural* one, for can it be denied that we are all born thieves? I know at least that I was, and I suspect you were no better. If you are not a thief now, it's because you were by good monitors twisted and torn out of that devil's form; and how much pains were taken to get you into another, so that it is only at best a second nature with you to be honest. In short, the thief is a more natural being than you are, although you think him a monster. Nor is it any wonder he's perfect, for your laws and habits have only wrought as a direct help of the character he got from the mother of us all, and probably his own mother in particular. Any obstruction he meets with is, therefore, something that ought to give way, simply because it shouldn't be there; for how can you prove to him that an act of parliament has greater authority than the instinct with which he was born. No doubt he won't argue with you. If you say you have a right to lock up, he won't say that he has a right to unlock down, but he'll do it, and not only without compunction, but with the same feeling of right that the tiger has when he seizes on an intruder upon the landmarks of his jungle and tears him to pieces.

On proceeding to Coates Crescent, I ascertained that the thieves had obtained entrance by opening the outer main door with keys or pick-locks, and all the rest was easy. The scene inside was just what Mr Jackson had described it—there wasn't a lock to an escritoire or drawer that was not punched off. Every secret place intended for holding valuables had been searched; and it soon appeared that these *artistes* had been very assiduous, if not a long time at the work. It would not be easy for me to enumerate the booty—valuable gold rings, earrings with precious stones, brooches of fine material and workmanship, silver ornaments of price, pieces of plate, and articles of foreign bijouterie. They had wound up with things they stood in need of for personal wear—top coats, boots, and stockings; and, to crown all, as many bottles of fine wine as would suffice to make a jolly bout when they reached their home. I have not mentioned a small musical box, because by bringing it in as I now do at the end, I want to lay some stress upon it, to the effect of getting it to play a tune.

I soon saw that I had a difficult case in hand, and I told Mr Jackson as much. The thieves were of the regular mould. I had no personal traces to trust to, and the articles taken away were of so meltable or transferable a nature that it might not be easy to trace them. My best chance lay in the articles of dress, for, as I have already hinted, thieves deriving their right from nature have all a corresponding ambition to be gentlemen. There's something curious here. Those who work their way up by honest industry seldom think of strutting about in fine clothes. Social feelings have taken the savage out of 'em. It is the natural-born gentleman who despises work that adorns our promenades and ball-rooms. 'Tis because they have a diploma from nature; and so the thieves who work by natural instinct come slap up to them and claim an equality. Certain it is, anyhow, I never knew a regular thief who didn't think he was a gentleman, and as for getting him to forego a nobby coat from a pin, he would almost be hanged first. I have found this my cue pretty often.

I had, therefore, some hope from the coats, but while getting a description of them and the other articles I felt a kind of curiosity about the peculiarities of the musical box.

"A small thing," said Mr Jackson, "some six inches long and three broad."

"Too like the others of its kind," said I; and giving way to a whim at the moment, "What tunes does it play?"

"Why, I can hardly tell," replied he, "for it belongs rather to the females. But I think I recollect that 'The Blue-Bells of Scotland' is among them."

"Perhaps," said I, keeping up the humour of the thing, "I may thereby get an answer to the question, 'Where, tell me where, does my highland laddie dwell?'"

Mr Jackson smiled even in the midst of the wreck of his house.

"I fear," he said, "that unless you have some other clue than the tune, you won't get me back my property."

"I have done more by less than a tune," said I, not very serious, but without giving up my hope, which I have never done in any case till it gave up me.

So with my list completed, and a promise to the gentleman that independently of the joke about the box I would do my best to get hold of the robbers, as well as the property, I left him. I felt that it was not a job to be taken lightly, or rather, I should say, that I considered my character somewhat at stake, insomuch as the gentleman seemed to place faith in my name. There is an amount of routine in all inquiries of this kind. The brokers, the "big uncles", (the large pawns,) and the "half uncles", (the wee pawns,) were all to be gone through, and they were with that dodging assiduity so necessary to the success of our calling. No trace in these places, and as for seeing one of my natural gentlemen in a grand blue beaver top-coat, I could encounter no such figure. I not only could not find where my highland laddie dwelt, but I did not even know my lover. Nor did I succeed any better with those who are fond of rings, for that the jewellery had found its way among the Fancies I had little doubt. How many very soft hands I took hold of in a laughing way, to know whether they were jewelled with my cornelians or torquoises, I can't tell; but then their confidence as yet wanted the ripening of time, and I must wait upon a power that has no pity for detectives any more than for lovers.

And I did wait, yet not so long as that the tune of "The Blue-Bells of Scotland" had passed away, scared though it was by the hoarse screams and discords of crime and misery. One evening I was on the watch-saunter, still the old dodging way by which I have earned more than ever I did by sudden jerks of enthusiasm. I turned down Blackfriars' Wynd, and proceeded till I came to the shop of Mr Henry Devlin, who kept in that quarter a tavern, which, without reproach to the landlord, was haunted by those gentlemen who owe so much to nature. Now, I pray you, don't think I am a miracle-monger. I make the statement deliberately, and defy your suspicions when I say, that just as I came to the door of the tavern, which was open, and by the door of which I could see into a small room off the bar, my attention was arrested by a low and delicate sound. I placed my head by the edge of the open door and listened. The sound was that of a musical box. The tune was so low and indistinct that I held my breath, as if thereby I could increase the watchful-ness of my ear. "It is! it is!" I muttered. Yes, it was "The Blue-Bells of Scotland". The charmed instrument ceased; and so enamoured had I been for the few seconds, that I found myself standing in the attitude of a statue for minutes after the cause of my enchantment had renounced its power.

With a knowledge of what you here anticipate, I claim the lib-erty of a pause, to enable me to remark, that though utterly unfit to touch questions of so ticklish a nature, I have had reason to think, in my blunt way, that in nine cases out of ten there is something mysterious in the way of Providence towards the discovery of crime. Just run up the history of almost any detective you please, and you will come to the semblance of a trace so very minute that you may view it either as a natural or a mysterious thing, just according to your temperament and your point of view. As a philosopher, and a little hardened against the supernatural, you may treat my credulity as you think proper. I don't complain, provided you admit that I am entitled to my weakness; but bearing in mind at the same time, that there are always working powers which make a considerable fool of our reasoning. Take it as you may, and going no further than the musical box, explain to me how I should have that night gone down Blackfriars' Wynd, and came to Henry Devlin's door just as "The Blue-Bells of Scotland" was being played by that little bit of machinery. You may go on with your thoughts as I proceed to tell you, that recovering myself from my surprise I entered the house. I did not stop at the bar where Mrs Devlin was, but proceeded direct into the room into which I could see from the door, and there, amidst empty tankards, I found the little instrument which had so entranced me, mute and tuneless, just as if it had been conscious that it had done some duty imposed upon it, and left the issue to the Power that watches over the fortunes of that ungrateful creature, man.

Taking up the monitor, which on the instant became dead to me.

"How came this here?" I said to the landlady, who seemed to be watching my movements.

"Indeed, I can hardly tell, Mr M'Levy," replied she, "unless it was left by the twa callants wha were in drinking, and gaed out just before you cam in. Did you no meet them?"

"No."

"Then they maun hae gaen towards the Cowgate as you cam by the High Street."

I paused an instant as an inconsistency occurred to me.

"But they couldn't have forgotten a thing that was making sounds at the very moment they left?"

"Aye, but they did though," replied the woman. "The thing had been kept playin' a' the time they were drinking, and was playin' when they paid their score, and the sound being drowned in the clatter o' the payment, they had just forgotten it even as I did. It plays twa or three tunes," she added, "and among the lave 'The Blue-Bells of Scotland', a tune I aye liked, for ye ken I'm Scotch."

"And I like it too," replied I, "though I'm Irish; but do you know the lads?"

"Weel—I do, and I dinna. Ane o' them has been here afore, and if you were to mention his name, I think I could tell you if it was the right ane."

"Shields," said I.

"The very name," said she, "and if I kenned whaur he lived I would send the box to him."

"I will save you that trouble, Mrs Devlin," said I, as I put it in my pocket.

"I never took you for a thief, Mr M'Levy," said she, in a half humorous way. "I aye took ye for a thief catcher."

"And it's just to catch the thief I take the box," said I. "You can speak to the men if I bring them here?"

"Brawly."

And so I left the tavern. I had got my trace, and knew where to go for my men, and I had, moreover, a well-grounded suspicion not only as regarded him whose name I had mentioned, but also his companion. I sent immediately for two constables, and having procured these, and been joined by my assistant, I proceeded to Brodie's Close in the Cowgate. Arriving at the foot of a stair, I planted there my constables, and mounted till I came to a door familiar to me on prior occasions.

I gave my quiet knock,—a signal so regular, that, as I have sometimes heard, it was known as "M'Levy's warning". Whether known as such now, or not, I cannot say, but it was quickly enough responded to by no less a personage than the famous Lucky Shields herself. The moment she saw me she recoiled, but only for an instant, and then tried to detain me—the ordinary sign that I should

be in. Without saying a word I pushed her back, and making my
way forward, got at once into the middle of one of those scenes of
which the quiet normal people of the world have no more idea than
they have of what is going on in the molten regions of the middle of
the earth, on the surface of which they are plucking roses. A large
room, where the grandees of a former time drank their claret to the
tune of "Lewie Gordon"; all about the sides a number of beds—
one or two rattled up of pine stumps—another with black carved
legs, which had supported fair dames long since passed away, alongside another with no more pretensions to decayed grandeur than
could be put forth by a sack of chaff and a horse-cloth. Close to that
a ragged arm-chair, with a bundle of hay rolled up in an old napkin,
to serve when there was an additional lodger. A number of chairs,
marrowless, broken, and rickety; a white table in the midst of all,
covered with glasses and tankards, all replete with the ring of drinking echoes, and shining in the haze of tobacco smoke, illuminated
by bright gas.

My ears were more bewildered than my eyes; for the room, with
its strange furniture, was familiar enough to me; but I had some
difficulty for a minute or two in distinguishing the living articles.
Round the fir table sat my hero of the box, Patrick Shields; alongside of him, Henry Preger,—so true an associate of Shields, as to
render it impossible for me to doubt his participation in the affair
at Coates Crescent; and along with these Daniel O'Hara, a gentleman with a peculiar turn of thought, which induced him to believe
that a watch in another man's pocket was out of its proper place.
The two first were still fuming with the effects of Mrs Devlin's whisky,
and O'Hara seemed to be great, as master of the new-brewed
potation, whisky-punch, which he had been handing round to the
young women. I don't want to paint vividly, in my slap dash way,
where picturesqueness is only to be effected at the expense of the
decencies of life, and you don't want pictures of vice. Then, what
boots it to describe such women. Their variety is only a combination of traces which are as uniform as the features of sensuality.
Yes, these young women, who were quite familiar to me—Agnes

Marshall, Jessie Ronald, Elizabeth Livingstone, Hannah Martin, Julia Shields—were simply representatives of thousands bearing the same marks,—one, a demure but cunning catcher of hearts and purses; another, a fair and comely living temple, with a Dagon of vice stuck up in it; another, never sober except when in a police cell, and never silent except when asleep, and scarcely then, for I have heard the cry of her wild spirit as it floated in drunken dreams; and another, the best resetter in the city, from whom a century of years in prison would not have extorted a Brummagem ring of the value of a glass of whisky. If I force so much of a picture upon you, it is because, as a part of society, you deserve to know what your laws and usages produce.

It was not for a little time after I entered that the confusion of tongues ceased. Their spirits had received such an impetus from the effects of the spirituous, that the speed could not be stopped; and even when the noise was hushed, it was only after the muttering of oaths. Meanwhile, a glance told me I had got into the very heart of the reset-box of Mr Jackson's fine jewellery. Finger and ear-rings glittered in the gas-light, and the expensive coats, at the top of the fashion, made Shields and Preger look like gentlemen who had called in from Princes Street to see the jewelled beauties. I have always had my own way of dealing with such gentry. I took out my musical box, and pulling the string, set it agoing. I have heard of music that drew stones—mine drew bricks. Shields and Preger fixed their eyes wildly upon me; and the women, who knew nothing of the meaning of M'Levy's music, first shot out into a yell of laughter, and then, rising, began, in the madness of their drunkenness, to dance like so many furies, keeping time, so far as they could, to the tune of the instrument. I could account for this insensibility to danger by no other way than by supposing that they had not previously seen the box, and did not see the consequences that were likely to result from my visit.

After the hubbub ceased, I addressed my man in the first instance.

"Patrick," said I, "I am come to return your box."

"It's not mine," replied the youth; "I have nothing to do with it."

"It's mine anyhow," cried the unwary mother, who all this time was looking through the smoke like a tigress. "The spaking thing is mine anyhow, for didn't me own Julia get it from a raal gintleman to learn her to sing, and isn't what's hers mine?"

And how much more of this Irish howl I might have heard, I can't say, if the son had not shot a look into her which brought her to a sense of her imprudence.

"And it's not my box afther all, ye vagabond," she cried, in trying to retreat from her error: "for wasn't mine an ivory one, and didn't it play real Irish tunes? Come here, Julia; is that your box?"

"No," said Julia.

"And wasn't yours raal ivory?"

"Yes," replied the girl.

"Now, didn't I tell you, you murtherin' thief, it wasn't my box. A way wid you, and never show your ugly face here again among dacent people."

The ordinary gabble of all such interviews. I gave a nod, to my assistant, and in a few minutes the constables were at my back.

"Well," said I, addressing the men, "you can carry the top-coats on your backs to the office; but as for you, ladies, there are certain finger and ear ornaments about you which, for fear you lose them, I must take."

These few simple words quieted the turmoil in an instant. I have often produced the same effect by a quiet exercise of authority. The boisterousness of vice, with no confidence to support it, runs back and oppresses the heart, which has no channel for it in the right direction; the channel has been long dried and seared.

"Search them," said I.

A process which, as regards women, we generally leave to our female searchers, but which I was obliged to have recourse to here in a superficial way to guard valuables, so easily secreted or cast away, and a process which requires promptness even to the instant; for on such an occasion, the cunning of women is developed with a subtlety transcending all belief. The hair, the hollow of the cheek, under the tongue, in the ear, up the nostrils, even the stomach being often resorted to as the receptacles of small but valuable articles. We contrived all four to dart upon the creatures at once, each seizing his prey. The suddenness of the onset took them by surprise, and in the course of a few minutes, we had collected into a shining heap nearly the whole of Mr Jackson's most valuable jewels.

We then marched the whole nine up to the Police-Office, I carrying the magic box, which, if I had been vainglorious, I would have set agoing as an appropriate accompaniment to our march up the High Street.

They were all tried on the 25th July 1843; Preger got fourteen years, and Shields ten. The women got off on the admission that they got the jewellery from Shields and Preger. I remember that, after the trial, Mr Jackson addressed me something in these terms:—

"Mr M'Levy, I owe the recovery of my property to you. I will retain my jewels, but as for the articles of apparel, I am afraid that were I to wear them I might myself become a thief; so you may dispose of them, and take the proceeds, with my thanks. The musical box I will keep as a useful secret informer; so that in the event of my house being robbed again, it may have a chance, through its melody, of recovering my property."

The Broker's Secret

❖

I have often heard it said that the past part of my life must have been a harassing and painful one; called on, as my reputation grew, in so many cases,—obliged to get up at midnight, to pursue thieves and recover property in so wide a range as a city with 200,000 inhabitants, and often with no clue to seize, but obliged in so many instances, to trust to chance. All this is true enough, and yet in fails in being a real description, insomuch as it leaves out the incidents that maintain and cheer the spirit,—for I need scarcely say, that if any profession now-a-days can be enlivened by adventure, it is that of a detective officer. With the enthusiasm of the sportsman, whose aim is merely to run down and destroy often innocent animals, he is impelled by the superior motive of benefiting mankind, by ridding society of pests, and restoring the broken fortunes of suffering victims; but, in addition to all this, his ingenuity is taxed while it is solicited by the sufferers, and replayed by the applause of a generous public. A single triumph of ingenuity has repaid me for many a night's wandering and searching, with not even a trace to guide me.

On the 28th of September 1848, the house of Mr Gravat, butcher in Hanover Street, was entered in the forenoon, by keys, and a large quantity of jewellery and article of clothing were abstracted. I got immediate notice; and having examined the people who saw the thieves coming out of the stair, I was enabled, from my general knowledge of almost all the members of the tribe—at that time, though only twelve years ago, so much more numerous than now—to fix upon my men. I have made the cheering remark "so much more numerous then than now," and it is suggestive of a consideration.

Society itself has always made its own pests, and it astonishes one to think how long we have been in coming in to this thought,—nay, it is comparatively only a few years old, as if we had been always blind to the fact, that there are two kinds of thieves and robbers: one comprising those that have no choice but to continue their early habits, got from their parents and associates, and who are wicked from the necessities of their position; the others, those that are born outlaws. The latter are not so numerous as one would imagine, and though, from their natures, independent from any care or culture, could be easily managed. To reclaim is nearly out of the question; but a speculation on that subject is beyond my depth, my duty being to catch them, and get them punished. But I repeat that I don't believe they are so numerous as is generally thought. As for the other class, let our Social Science friends just act up to the modern invention of anticipating the natural wants of human creatures, and the numbers of thieves and robbers will diminish further still.

The young men engaged in the robbery I have just mentioned were just a part of these pests which we have been making for ourselves, by allowing parents to do what they like with their children,—a privilege we don't allow to the masters of dogs, which, if they show a tendency to be dangerous, may be laid hold of before they bite. Yes, Alexander M'Kay, David Hunter, and Thomas Ogilvy, who committed the robbery, and whom I apprehended, would probably have never been in my hands if they had been simply put to a trade, though the medium of a ragged school, or some other mean of that kind of benevolence; which is a duty to society itself. I had got my lads,—for men they could hardly be said to be,—but where was the jewellery? The mere fact of their having been seen coming out of Mr Gravat's stair was not enough even for a small supplement to habit and repute, if it was anything more than a trace to discover them by.

I therefore set about the discovery of the jewels and clothes,—a far more difficult task, if the thieves are cunning, than the seizure of their persons,—and here I found myself at fault, notwithstanding the most unwearied trudging amongst brokers, resetters, houses of bad fame, and inquiries and searches into even the most unlikely places, not a ring or even a handkerchief could I find, so that I was fast arriving at the conclusion that the articles had been "planked", as they call it, somewhere, perhaps in the outskirts of the town, behind a hedge, or under the ground, or in some of the many holes and boles about the old town, left by the gentry, it would almost seem, for the accommodation of their successors. I must try another mode. I have often succeeded in getting young offenders to be communicative. Though all adepts at using their fingertips, they are not so adroit in using, or rather not using, their tongues. One of the three,—Hunter,—seemed to me to be a likely blabber, if I could once set the instrument a-going. Having got him by myself,—

"Now, Hunter," I said, "I want you to tell me where those things are you and your friends took out of Mr Gravat's house."

"Know nothing about them;"—the old story.

"Well, I'll convict you, anyhow," said I; "a single handkerchief will do the job; you know you have been 'up' before, and it don't take much in that case."

"But you haven't got the handkerchief," said he, as he began to watch my face.

"Don't be too sure," I said, as I noticed some sign of his being, at least, apprehensive. "I think you know I seldom fail."

He was silent, but not dogged.

"I will be your friend", I continued, "and make you a witness."

His eye began to gather some light. "What do you want?"

"Just to tell me where the stolen things are, no more. I don't want you to confess that you were one of the robbers."

"Do you not? And you will make me a witness?"

"I think I will manage that for you, if you don't deceive me."

He thought for a while. "But I wouldn't have the life of a dog were I known as a peacher."

"I'll take care of you; don't be afraid, and something may be done for you."

Still doubts, and still the terror of being set upon by the gang. I could not help pitying the condition of these slaves to a tyranny that leaves them no chance of penitence or amendment; but seeing the turning-point—the assurance of security—he was easily screwed up, yet I was, by his very first words of disclosure, discomfited. Looking up in my face,—

"It's no use," he said.

"What do you mean?" I replied, as I noticed something like a mysterious look about him.

"Why, the things," said he, as if it was a revelation of something very dark, "are beyond the reach of anyone. Hamilton has got them, and we all know that when he has them they can never be found."

"That's Hamilton the hawing broker in the Canongate," said I.

"Yes, but you don't know," he continued, "that Hamilton has a secret place in his house, which no man has ever found, and nobody will ever find, where he puts all the stolen articles he gets, and, I tell you, you'll never find them."

"Where is the secret place?"

"I don't know. Nobody knows but himself and his wife."

"You are certain it is within the house?"

"Yes."

"And if you cannot tell I which part of the house it is, nor what kind of place it is, whether above ground or under, how do you come to know of it at all?"

"I cannot tell how it came to be known," said he; all I can say is, that it is a secret among us."

It now flashed upon me that this man, Thomas Hamilton, had been long able to put us at fault; and the information I now got explained to me his way of doing business. He was thought to be rich, and rich he might well be, from a lucrative trade said to have been so well conducted. He was known to be a hawker as well as broker, going about the country, and disposing of articles which he could not have exposed in Edinburgh; and having this secret place of deposit, whereby he could, as he so often had done, elude our diligent search, he was always at his ease. I had no doubt he had carried on his system for a long period, and been enabled not only to save a deal of money, but to preserve among the fraternity, or rather sisterhood, of brokers a fair reputation.

Taking four men with me to watch, in case, upon my disturbing the secret fountain, some streams might take to running outside, I went in upon Mr Hamilton, whom I found in his lower place of business, among those piles of furniture and other things which form so peculiar a feature of a broker's shop in the Canongate. He knew me too well, and did not require to tell my errand; yet, though perfectly aware that I had come, as many had done before, to search his house, he betrayed no fear; if, indeed, he did not appear perfectly indifferent.

"You are quite welcome," he said; "I don't think you will find any property here that has been stolen."

I saw no necessity for a reply to a statement which I was in the habit of hearing every day, and silently commenced my survey through the shop or warehouse. I saw nothing there to take my fancy, though one might have supposed that a mass of furniture was a very good covering for a concealed hole in the floor, and I might recur to that if I failed elsewhere. The only thing that I envied was a hammer lying within reach; and, taking it up,

"Excuse me, said I.

"You may say so," said he; "for I made that except the head with my own hands."

"Oh, I'll not injure it," I rejoined.

He did not seem to understand this proceeding at all, but he never lost for a moment his confidence, if there was not rather a faint smile on his face, just as if he thought, "oh, you're vastly clever, but I'm a-head of you."

I then proceeded up an inside stair, which communicated between the shop and the dwelling-house above, followed by my man, who led me into a sitting room. I expected nothing from a place into which I was *led*, but I did not object to look about me, which I did very cursorily.

"Where is your bed-room?" I inquired, as I turned and went to a closet door. "This will be it, I fancy?"

"Ay," drily, and to me hopefully.

On entering, I immediately began, without a moment's notice, to apply the hammer to the wall, continuing my soundings gradually along over the fire-place, and on the next wall, and on and on till I came to where the bed stood. It had curtains on it,—and here the weakness of vice, as usual, betrayed itself by its whispering revelations: Hamilton became uneasy about his bed, held up the side curtains against the wall, and said, "Nothing there you see."

"I didn't expect anything in the bed, Mr Hamilton," said I, "but please let the curtain fall till I see if the wall is all sound and healthy over the top of the bed, it may come down and bury you and your wife some morning."

A grim smile followed my remark, and I could have read the fate of my enterprise in his face. I continued my soundings, till, after half-a-hundred dull and very unsatisfactory answers, there was one which thrilled through me, and I have no doubt, Hamilton also. Perhaps he had never in all his life heard any sound so like that produced by the shovelful of mould on the coffin-lid. Yet, so differently do we estimate things, it was to me more like the ringing of a marriage-bell.

"You're not sound here, just at this spot, Mr Hamilton; and then, to think it is quite over the head of your bed, where you and Mrs Hamilton sleep so innocently after the day's toil."

On getting a chair and mounting, I observed a slight ruffle on the paper,—a part of that which covered all the four walls,—and, examining still more minutely, I thought I observed a very thin fine crack, appearing as if a knife had been brought along it to the extent of a couple of inches. I then took out a small penknife, inserted it into the crack, gave it a slight pressure down, and out started a very miniature door, which, on afterwards measuring, I found to be 8 inches by 6. It had a very peculiar and ingeniously-made hinge, on which it went so secretly, that the paper over it appeared to be entire.

" A regular pigeon-hole, Mr Hamilton," said I; "what is the use of this?"

"I never knew there was such a hole there," he said; "it must have been made and left by the last tenant."

"Who has perhaps left some jewels in it," I rejoined; and, putting in my hand, I pulled out a very valuable gold watch.

"A good beginning," I said, as I laid it on the bed. My next handful was a parcel containing a great portion of Mr Gravat's jewellery.

"Quite a pose," I continued, as I now laid that down; "there's no use in people going so far for gold, when one can dig it out here with a penknife."

And proceeding in the same way with all proper and decorous deliberation, I pulled handful after handful of all kinds of valuable things, from gold time-pieces to tiny rings, till I emptied the large jewel-box and covered the bed.

"And now, Mr Hamilton, have you any large box or trunk about you, of small value, which you can lend me for an hour, to contain these things, and then my men will take them up to the Police-office?"

"They must all have belonged to the last tenant," he persisted in saying, as he turned out to comply with my request.

Presently he brought in a chest, and then I called in two of my men, who soon got the valuables packed, and carried them away.

"There are just two other jewels I want," said I,—you and your wife."

And, calling the other men, we marched the couple—the wife having come in, and been below, wondering what all their work was about—up to the office.

The parties were all brought to trial except Hunter. Hamilton was sentenced to seven years' transportation, and the two lads to eighteen months' imprisonment. The wife was acquitted on the plea that she was under the command and influence of the husband.

No one can say that the fate of Hamilton was too severe. His resetship was probably not more criminal than the others, but the effect, in giving confidence to young men sufficiently inclined to their evil ways otherwise, aggravated his case. I believe that the common remark that the resetter is worse than the thief, and upon which our judges proceed, is correct, if it may not, indeed, be nearly self-evident; for while he in effect makes the thieves, he profits more than they, and besides, escapes the risks of personal danger.

The Dead Child's Leg

Some years ago, the scavenger whose district lies about the Royal Exchange, came to the office in a state of great excitement. He had a parcel in his hand, and laying it on the table, said, "I've found something this morning you won't guess."

"A bag of gold, perhaps?" said I.

"I wish it had been," said the man, looking at the parcel, a dirty rolled-up napkin, with increased fear; "it's a bairn's leg."

"A bairn's leg!" said I, taking up the parcel, and undoing it with something like a tremor in my own hand, which had never shaken when holding by the throat such men as Adam M'Donald.

And there, to be sure, was a child's leg, severed about the middle of the thigh. On examining it, it was not difficult to see that it was a part of a new-born infant, and a natural curiosity suggested a special look to the severed end, to know what means had been taken to cut it from the body. The result was peculiar. It appeared as if a hatchet had been applied to cut the bone, and that the operator had finished the work by dragging the member from the body,— a part of the muscle and integuments looking lacerated and torn. The leg was bleached, as if it had lain in water for a time, and it was altogether a ghastly spectacle.

"Where did you find it?" I asked.

"Why," replied the man, "I was sweeping about in Writers' Court at gray dawn, and, with a turn of my broom, I threw out of a sewer something white; then it was so dark I was obliged to stoop down to get a better look, and the five little toes appeared so strange that I staggered back, knowing very well now what it was. But I have always been afraid of dead bodies. Then I tied it up in my handkerchief, more to conceal it from my own sight than for any other reason."

"And you can't tell where it came from?" said I.

"Not certainly," answered he; "but I have a guess."

And the man, an Irishman, looked very wise, as if his guess was a very dark ascertained reality, something terribly mysterious.

"Out with your guess, man," said I; "it looks like a case of murder, and we must get at the root of it."

"And I will be brought into trouble," answered he; "faith, I'll say no more. I've given you the leg, and that's pretty well, anyhow. It's not every day you get the like o' that brought to ye, all for nothing; and ye're not content."

"You know more than you have told us," said I; "and how are we to be sure that you did not put the leg there yourself?"

"Put the leg there myself, and then bring it to you!" said he; "first kill the bairn, and then come to be hanged! Not just what an Irishman would do. We're not so fond of trouble as all that."

"Trouble or no trouble, you must tell us where you think it came from, otherwise we will detain you as a suspected murderer."

"Mercy save us! me a suspected murderer!" cried he, getting alarmed; "well now, to be plain, you see, the leg was lying just at the bottom of the main soil-pipe that comes from the whole of the houses on the east side of the court, and it must be somebody in some family in some flat in some house in some part of the row that's the mother,—that's pretty certain; and I think I have told you enough to get at the thief of a mother."

The man, no doubt, pointed at the proper source, however vaguely; so taking him along with me I walked over to Writers' Court, and, after examining the place where the leg was found, I was in some degree satisfied the man was right. I was exceedingly unlikely that the member would be thrown down there by any one entering the court, or by any one from a window, for this would just have been to exhibit a piece of evidence that a murder, or at least a concealed birth had taken place somewhere in the neighbourhood, and to send the officers of the law upon inquiry. Besides, the leg was found in the gutter leading from the main pipe of the tenements, and, though there was no water flowing at the time there had been a sufficiency either on the previous night or early morning to wash it to where it had lain.

But after coming to this conclusion, the difficulty took another shape, not less unpromising. The pipe, as the man truly said, was a main pipe, into which all the pipes of the different houses led. One of these houses was Mr W—te's inn, which contained several females, and the other divisions of flats had each its servant; but, in addition to all this there were females of a higher grade throughout the lands, and I shrunk from an investigation so general, and carrying an imputation so terrible. My inquiry was not to be among people of degraded character, where a search or a charge was only a thing of course,—doing no harm where they could not be more suspected than they deserved,—but among respectable families, some with females of tender feelings, regardful of a reputation which, to be suspected, was to be lost for ever; and I required to be on my guard against precipitation and imprudence.

Yet my course so far was clear enough. I could commit no imprudence, while I might expect help, in confining my first inquiries to the heads of the families; and this I had resolved upon while yet standing in the court in the hazy morning. The man and I were silent—he sweeping, and I meditating—when, in the stillness which yet prevailed, I heard a window drawn up in that stealthy way I am accustomed to hear when crime is on the outlook. It was clear that the greatest care had been taken to avoid noise; but ten times the care, and a bottle of oil to boot, would not have enabled this morning watcher to escape my ear. On the instant I slipt into an entry, the scavenger still sweeping away, and, notwithstanding of his shrewdness, not alive to an important part of the play. I could see without being seen; and looking up, I saw a white cap with a young and pale face under it, peering down upon the court. I had so good a look of the object, that I could have picked out that face, so peculiar was it, from among a thousand. I could even notice the eye, nervous and snatchy, and the secret-like movement of withdrawing the head as she saw the man, and then protruding it a little again as she observed him busy. Then there was a careful survey, not to ascertain the kind of morning, or to converse with a neighbouring protruded head, but to watch, and see, and hear what was going on below, where probably she had heard the voices of me and the man. Nay, I could have sworn that she directed her eye to the conduit—a suspicion on my part which afterwards appeared to me to be absurd, as in the event of her being the criminal, and knowing the direction of the pipes, she never would have trusted her life to such an *open* mode of concealment as sending the mutilated body down through the inside pipes, to be there exposed.

After looking anxiously and timidly for some time, and affording me, as I have said, sufficient opportunity to scan and treasure up her features, she quietly drew in her pale, and, as I thought, beautiful face, let down the sash, almost with a long whisper of the wood, and all was still. I now came out of my hiding-place, and telling the man not to say a word to any one of what had been seen or done, I went round to the Exchange, and satisfied myself of the house thus signalised by the head of the pale watcher of the morning.

I need not say I had my own thoughts of this transaction but still I saw that to have gone and directly impeached this poor, timid looker-out upon the dawn for scarcely any other reason than she did then and there look out, and that she had a delicate appearance, would have been unauthorised, and perhaps fraught with painful consequences. What if I had failed in bringing home to her a tittle of evidence, and left her with a ruined reputation for life? The thought alarmed me, and I behoved to be careful, however strict, in the execution of my duty; so I betook myself during the forenoon to my first resolution of having conferences with the heads of the houses.

I took the affair systematically, beginning at one end and going through the families. No master or mistress could I find who could say they had observed any *signs* in any of their female domestics. The last house was a reservation—that house from which my watcher of the morning had been intent upon the doings in the court. It was the inn occupied, as I have said, by Mr W—te. Strangely enough, the door was opened by that same pale-faced creature. I threw my eye over her,—the same countenance, delicate and interesting,— the same nervous eye, and look of shrinking fear,—but now a smart cap on her head, which was like a mockery of her sadness and melancholy. She eyed me curiously and fearfully as I asked for Mr W—te, and ran with an irregular and irresolute motion to show me in. I made no inquiry of her further, nor did I look at her intently to rouse her suspicion, for I had got all I wanted, even that which a glance carried to me. But if she showed me quickly in, I could see that she had no disposition to run away when the door of the room opened. No doubt she was about the outside of it. I took care she could learn nothing there, but few will ever know what she had suffered there.

I questioned Mr W—te confidentially; told him all the circumstances; and ended by inquiring whether any of his female domestics had shown any *signs* for a time bypast.

"No," said he; "such a thing could hardly have escaped me; and if I had suspected, I would have made instant inquiry, for the credit of my house."

"What is the name of the young girl who opened the door to me?"

"Mary B——n, but I cannot allow myself to suspect her; she is a simple-hearted, innocent creature, and is totally incapable of such a thing."

"But is she not pale and sickly-looking as if some such event as that I allude to might have taken place in her case?"

"Why, yes; I admit," said he, "that she is paler than she used to be, but she has been often so while with me; and then her conduct is so circumspect, I cannot listen to the suspicion."

"Might I see the others?" said I.

"Certainly;" replied he, "I can bring them here upon pretences."

"You may, except Mary B——n," said I; "I have seen enough of her."

And Mr W——te brought up several females on various pretences, all of whom I surveyed with an eye not more versed in these indications than what a very general knowledge of human nature might have enabled one to be. Each of them bore my scrutiny well and successfully—all healthy, blithe queans, with neither blush nor paleness to show anything wrong about the heart or conscience.

"All these are free," said I, "but I must take the liberty to ask you to show me the openings to the soil-pipe belonging to the tenement, but in such a way as not to produce suspicion; for I think you will find Mary about the door of the room."

And so it turned out, for no sooner had we come forth than we could see the poor girl escaping by the turn of the lobby.

"*That is my lass*," said I to myself.

The investigation of the pipes showed me nothing. There was not in any of the closets a drop of blood, nor sign of any kind of violence to a child, nor in any bed-room a trace of birth, and far less a murder; but I could not be driven from my theory. My watcher of the morning of day was she who had taken the light of the morning of life from the new-born babe.

I consulted with the police doctor, and he saw at once difficulties of the case. The few facts, curious and adventitious as they were, which had come under my own eye, were almost for myself alone; no other would have been moved by them because they might have been supposed to be coloured by my own fancy. Yet I felt I had a case to make out in some way, however much the reputation of a poor young girl should implicated, and not less my own character and feelings. As yet, proof there was none. To have taken up a girl merely because she had a pale face—the only indication I could point to that others could judge of—was not according to my usual tactics; but I could serve my purpose without injuring the character of the girl were she innocent, and yet convict her if guilty. So I thought; and my plan, which was my own, was, as a mere tentative one, free from the objection of hardship or cruelty to the young woman.

About twelve o'clock I rolled up the leg of the child in neat paper parcel, and writing an address upon it to Mary B——n, at Mr W—te's, I repaired to the inn. Mary, who was not exclusively "the maid of the inn," did not this time open the door; it was done by one whose ruddy cheeks would have freed her from the glance of the keenest detective.

"Is Mary B——n in?" asked I.

"Yes," she replied somewhat carelessly; for I need not say there was not a suspicion in the house, except in the breast of Mr W—te, who was too discreet and prudent to have said a word.

"Tell her I have a parcel from the country to her," said I, walking in, and finding my way into a room.

The girl went for Mary, and I waited a considerable time; but then, probably, she might have been busy making the beds, perhaps her own, in a careful way, though she scarcely needed, after my eye had surveyed the sheets and blankets, as well as everything else. At length I heard some one at the door,—the hand not yet on the catch—a shuffling, a sighing, a flustering—the hand then applied and withdrawn—a sighing again—at length a firmer touch,—the door opened, and Mary stood before me. She was not pale now; a sickly flush overspread the lily—the lip quivered— the body swerved; she would have fallen had not she called up a little resolution not to betray herself.

"What—what—you have a parcel for me, sir?" she stuttered out.

"Yes, Mary," said I, as I still watched her looks, now changed again to pure pallor.

"Where is it from?" said she again, with still increased emotion.

"I do not know," said I, "but here it is," handing it to her.

The moment her hand touched it, she shrunk from the soft feel as one would do from that of a cold snake, or why should I not say the dead body of a child? It fell at her feet, and she stood motionless, as one transfixed, and unable to move even a muscle of the face.

"That is not the way to treat a gift," said I. "I insist upon you taking it up."

"O God, I cannot!" she cried.

"Well, I must do so for you," said I, taking up the parcel. Is that the way you treat the presents of your friends; come," laying it on the table, "come, open it; I wish to see what is in it."

"I cannot,—oh, sir, have mercy on me,—I cannot."

"Then do you *wish* me to do it for you?"

"Oh, no, no,—I would rather you took it away," she said with a spasm.

"But why so? what do you think is in it?" said I, getting more certain every moment of my woman.

"Oh, I do not know," she cried again; "but I cannot open that dreadful thing."

And as she uttered the words, she burst into tears, with a suppressed scream, which I was afraid would reach the lobby. I then went to the door, and snibbed it. The movement was still more terrifying to her, for she followed me, and grasped me convulsively by the arm. On returning to the table, I again pointed to the parcel.

"You must open that," said I, "or I will call in your master to do it for you."

"Oh,—for God's sake, no," she ejaculated; "I will,—oh yes, sir, be patient,—I will, I will."

But she didn't—she couldn't. Her whole frame shook, so that her hands seemed palsied, and I am sure she could not have held the end of the string.

"Well," said I, drawing in a chair, and seating myself, "shall wait till you are able."

The sight of the poor creature was now painful to me, but I had my duty to do, and I knew how much depended on her applying her own hand to this strange work. I sat peaceably and silently, my eye still fixed upon her. She got into meditation—looked piteously at me, then fearfully at the parcel—approached it—touched it—recoiled from it—touched it again and again—recoiled;—but I would wait.

"Why, what is all this about?" said I calmly, and I suspect even with a smile on my face, for I wanted to impart to her at least so much confidence as might enable her to do this one act, which I deemed necessary to my object. "What is all this about? I only bear this parcel to you, and for aught I know, there may be nothing in it to authorise all this terror. If you are innocent of crime, Mary, nothing should move you. Come, undo the string."

And now, having watched my face, and seen the good-humour on it, she began to draw up a little, and then picked irresolutely at the string.

"See," said I, taking out a knife, "this will help you."

But whether it was that she had been busy with a knife that morning for another purpose than cutting the bread for her breakfast, I know not; she shrunk from the instrument, and, rather than touch it, took to undoing the string with a little more resolution. And here I could not help noticing a change that came over her almost of a sudden. I have noticed the same thing in cases where necessity seemed to be the mother of energy. She began to gather resolution from some thought; and, as it appeared, the firmness was something like new-born energy to overcome the slight lacing of the parcel. That it was an effort bordering on despair, I doubt not, but it was not the less an effort. Nay, she became almost calm, drew the ends, laid the string upon the table, unfolded the paper, laid the object bare, and—the effort was gone—fell senseless at my feet.

I was not exactly prepared for this. I rose, and seeing some spirits in a press, poured out a little, wet her lips, dropped some upon her brow, and waited for her return to consciousness; and I waited longer than I expected,—indeed, I was beginning to fear I had carried my experiment too far. I thought the poor creature was dead, and for a time I took on her own excitement and fear, though from a cause so very different. I bent over her, watching her breath, and holding her wrist; at last a long sigh,—oh, how deep!—then a staring of the eyes, and a rolling of the pupils, then a looking to the table, then a rugging at me as if she thought I had her fate in my hands.

"Oh, where is it?" she cried. "Take it away; but you will hang me, will you? Say you will not, and I will tell you all."

I got her lifted up, and put upon a chair. She could now sit, but such was the horror she felt at the grim leg, torn as it was at the one end, and blue and hideous, that she turned her eyes to the wall, and I believe her smart cap actually moved by the rising of the black hair beneath it.

"Mary B———n," said I, calmly, and in a subdued voice, "you have seen what is in the parcel?"

"Oh, yes sir; oh, yes," she muttered.

"Do you know what it is?"

"Oh, too well, sir; too well."

"Then tell me," said I.

"Oh, sir," she cried, as she threw herself upon the floor on her knees, and grasped and clutched me round my legs and held up her face,—her eyes now streaming with tears, her cap off, her hair let loose,—"if I do, will you take pity on me, and not hang me?"

"I can say, at least, Mary," I replied, "that it will be better for you if you make a clean breast, and tell the truth. I can offer no promises. I am merely an officer of the law; but, as I have said, I know it will be better for you to speak the truth."

"Well, then, sir," she cried, while the sobbing interrupted every other word; "well, then, before God, whom I have offended, but who may yet have mercy upon a poor sinner left to herself,—and, oh, sir, seduced by a wicked man,—I confess that I bore that child—but, sir, it was dead when it came into the world; and, stung by shame, and wild with pain, I cut it into pieces, and put it down into the soil-pipe; and may the Lord Jesus look down upon me in pity!"

"Well, Mary," said I, as I lifted her up,—feeling the weight of a body almost dead,—and placed her again upon the chair; "you must calm yourself, and then go and get your shawl and bonnet, for you must—"

"Go with you to prison," she cried, "and be hanged. Oh, did you not lead me to believe you would save me?"

"No," said I; "but I can safely tell you that, if what you have told me is true, that the child was still-born, you will not be hanged, you will only be confined for a little. Come," I continued, letting my voice down, "come, rise, and get your shawl and bonnet. Say nothing to any one, but come back to me."

But I had not an easy task here. She got wild again at the thought of prison, crying—

"I am ruined. Oh, my poor mother! I can never look her in the face again; no, nor hold up my head among decent people."

"Softly, softly," said I. "You must be calm, and obey; or see," holding up a pair of handcuffs, "I will put these upon your wrists."

Again necessity came to my help. She rose deliberately—stood for a moment firm—looked into my face wistfully, yet mildly— then turned up her eyes, ejaculating, "Thy will, O Lord, be done,"— and went out.

I was afraid, notwithstanding, she might try to escape, for she seemed changeful; and a turn might come of frantic fear, which would carry her off, not knowing herself whither she went. I there-fore, watched in the lobby, to intercept her in use of such an emer-gency; but the poor girl was true to her purpose. I tied up the fatal parcel which had so well served my object, put it under my arm, and quietly led her over to the office.

Her confession was subsequently taken by the Crown officers, and she never swerved from it. I believe if I had not fallen upon this mode of extorting an admission, the proof would have failed, for every vestige of mark had been carefully removed; while the de-ception she had practised on the people of the inn had been so adroit, that no one had the slightest suspicion of her. The other parts of the child were not, I think, got; indeed it was scarcely necessary to search for them, confined as they were, probably, in the pipes. She was tried before the High Court; and, in the absence of an evidence to show that the child had ever breathed,—which could only have been ascertained by examining some parts of the chest,—she was condemned upon the charge of concealment, and sentenced to nine months' imprisonment.

A
Want
Spoils
Perfection

❖

The coming round of extremes, so as to meet and disappear in each other's ends, is a thing which all must have noticed, and why not I among the rest? I rather think that in my small way I couldn't have done what I have done, if I hadn't been a *thinker*, and so I have noticed the danger of overdoing things. Not only do strong passions, though good, land in the slough of evil, but overstretched prudence, cold and calculating, leads to a pretty considerable combustion. Yes, our old mother says, "Walk in the middle"—on the sides there are pitfalls; and yet we are never happy if we are not gaping over precipices, and talking of the picturesque and the sublime. No wonder a few topple over, and thus add to the picturesque.

When Mr C——, watchmaker in Arbroath, afraid as he was to leave his stock of watches in his shop, bethought himself of the prudent step of removing them at night, by a medium exposed to danger, he was just walking to the *side*. One night in January 1850, his two apprentices, in pursuance of their master's care, collected all the Watches—about fifty in number—with many other valuable things in silver and gold, and deposited them in a box, with the view of their being carried to Mr C——'s dwelling-house, at some distance from the shop. The shop was then locked up, and one of the lads, swinging the box on his back by means of a leather strap, proceeded, with his companion alongside of him as a guard, to the usual safe place of deposit. The night was pitch dark. Their way lay by a path where the houses were thinly scattered, and the property was thus placed in a far more dangerous position than if it had been left in a good safe under lock and key in the shop, also itself under lock and key, and all under the survey of neighbours—if not of the police. When some way on their road, up started two men, one of whom held the companion, while the other, applying a knife to the strap, undid the box and made off with it in an instant. The other, letting go his grip of the lad, was also off like a flash of lightning, and the extreme care of the valuable box was thus superseded by the effort of a few minutes. The boys were too much stunned to be able to pursue, even if they had had the courage, or even to bawl, though they had the common instinct, Like most other premeditated efforts, the thing was well done; and long before any hue and cry could be got up, the robbers were far away.

Next day the usual information came fulminating over to Edinburgh—usual, with the to-be-expected abatement, that no description could, in the circumstances, be possible. The boys, under the influence of the fear which paralysed them, could and did give nothing but a "travestie" of the features of the men. When I read the confused account,

"Why," said I to the Lieutenant, "these noses, eyes, and chins, are so like what we see every day, that I might as well take up the Lord Provost as any one else." And as I had been reading a funny satire of the man called Lavater, some nights before, I could not help being humorous in my own blunt way. "Do you know that a great man, Lichtenberg by name, a queer satirical body with a hunch, raised all Germany into a laugh, by publishing the figure of a pig with a nicely curled tail, and marked on one turn of the said tail 'firmness,' on another 'benevolence,' on another 'murder,' all of which went to show the nature of the animal, just as Lavater labelled the features of a man's face. So here we are required to find these two clever fellows, by signs given by two boys in the dark. I may find the watches, and thereby the men, and so far the intimation is proper and hopeful, but to expect us to find the men by their *noses*, is just rather too much."

"You can only do your best, James," said Mr Moxey, looking up at what he thought wonderfully learned in me.

"Yes, sir," replied I, "but I know no *best* but detection; without that the best is the worst."

So I could only try the usual places of deposit and pledge, when there might be time for the thieves getting here and disposing of their prey. Watches are "casting up" things. They are seldom melted, for their value is so much more than that of the materials, and then they are always in request, so I had some chance of meeting them somewhere—at least one or more out of such a stunning number as fifty. Accordingly, I did my best in the dead-object way, but without any success, and I could trust only to time and continual dodging to arrive at any discovery.

Some time passed, I don't remember how long. As for trying *faces*, it was out of the question, when I had neither image in my mind, or description to go by; and I need not say that I did not continue that, because I really never began it. But, as it will appear, my lucky genius had not flown away up above the stars to report how she had favoured me and had got enamoured of some other winged creatures, so as to delay her return. I was one night on my rounds in the Grassmarket, attended as usual by my companion. The night was not so dark as that one could not see a consider- able way before. I was rather complaining that there was nothing to see. We were approaching Smith's Close, when my ear was startled, and my eye directed towards a man who had instantane- ously left a companion, and rushed with clattering steps up the close.

"Seize that one," said I.

And after the other up the close I sprang at the top of my speed. I saw his dark figure before me, which, as the moon, getting from behind a cloud, threw a reflection, (made angular by the sky-line of the high houses,) came out in an instant, firm, clear, and distinct. There was no chance for him, and he knew it. She was not so kind to one of her "minions" on this occasion as she used to be in the old border times. Just as I was coming upon him, he whirled a guard from his neck and threw away a watch.

"What's the matter with the timepiece, man?" said I, as I laid hold of him, and dragging him to the article, picked it up. "Isn't it a good 'un that you threw it away?"

The fellow was sulky, and would not answer me; but a watch was so pleasant an object to me at that particular time that I overlooked the affront. Dragging him to the foot of the close, where his companion was in the custody of my assistant, we took our men to the Office, where I very soon discovered that the watch was one of Mr C——'s fifty. My anticipations, in which I had been so wise, were thus strangely enough reversed. In place of getting the men through the *watch*, I had got the watch through the *men*. And my next object was to improve upon the good fortune that had been so kind to me, in spite of my want of confidence in my benefactress. But here commenced a new difficulty. The men foolishly enough gave each the other's name, Alexander Clark and James Mitchell— quite different from those they carried for the nonce; but as for aught else, they were what we call lockmouths. No skeleton-key would reach their works. I was thus driven aback, nor did I make much progress for some time, except in hearing that one Hart had got another of the watches from another man, who had got it from Mitchell. This I, of course, treasured up in the meantime; but I was so anxious to worm out of my men where they resided—the true clue to all other discoveries—that I postponed all other inquiries, and besides, from what I knew of Hart, a lockmouth too, I had no hopes of him. All my efforts with my men were, however, vain. They would admit nothing as to their place of putting up; sullen, if not enraged, at the trick practised on them in getting each to give the other's real name. Why such men could have been so completely off their guard is not easy to be accounted for, except on the supposition that they were trying to fight shy of one another, or upon the principle I have often acted on, that even a cautious thief will sometimes allow the admission of a fact not directly implicating himself to be jerked out of him by a sudden question. After the men had been sent in custody to Dundee, I sought out Hart, and was just as unsuccessful with him. He would not admit to the watch, neither would he confess that he knew the residence of either the one or the other.

And here this strange case—destined to have so many crooks in its lot—took another turn, which, involving a little disregard of courtesy towards me, roused my independence to a rather grand vindication. The authorities in Dundee sent over an officer, who informed us that eighteen of the watches had been recovered there, and that they had ascertained, by the confession of Mitchell, that the thieves had been residing in Edinburgh, in a certain tavern kept by a Mrs Walker. Mr Moxey got the intelligence, and whether or not it was that he had been suddenly seized with the ambition of becoming a practical detective I cannot say; but true it is that, without any communication to me, he set out with the Dundee officer to find out Mrs Walker, and, no doubt, recover the remainder of the watches. Well, I allowed them full rope, and they wandered about for a whole day, without being able to find this same tavern. I knew very well what they were after, and could have led them to the house as direct as to the jail, but I abstained from all interference, where my services were, as I thought, superseded. Perhaps there was a little cunning—what could we do without it?— at the bottom of my very virtuous indignation.

At length, and when utterly exhausted, my superior called me in the evening.

"James," said he, "I can make nothing of this inquiry; there is no Mrs Walker's tavern in Edinburgh."

"Why, sir, hadn't you better continue the search all night? said I; "you may get the house before the morning."

He looked at me to see the state of my face, and smiled, for he was a very good-natured man.

"Do you mean what you recommend?" said he.

"To be sure I do," said I. "It was no wish of mine that you should begin the search, but seeing you have begun it, and every moment is precious, I think you should end it before you sleep."

"But I *have* ended it."

"Yes, in your way, but not exactly in mine. However, I am wearied, and, if you please, while you are *beginning* where you *ended*, I shall go to bed."

"I have done enough to-day," was the reply; "I shall see what more can be done tomorrow. I have some letters to write."

Leaving him, I went out, but in place of going down the High Street home, I proceeded to Smith's Close, where I knew Mrs Walker had her tavern, and had had it for years.

"Mrs Walker," said I, as the good woman opened the door, "did two young men lodge with you for a few days lately?"

"Ay," replied she.

"Will you show me where they slept?"

"Surely."

And leading the way, she showed me into a bedroom with one bed in it.

I then began to look about in my ordinary way, first very cursorily, and finding nothing, where I expected nothing, I got upon my knees, and sprawled in under the bed, so low being the bottom that it was with great difficulty I could get a part of my body in. I then came out again, as most people do when they get into any kind of holes, except one, pulling out after me a pillow-case, apparently, that is, to the touch, filled with hay, and so, to be sure, in undoing the mouth, I found it was. On pulling out the hay, however, I brought along with it a towel containing something hard.

"There will be eggs among the hay," said the landlady.

"Laid by *cocks*, perhaps," said I, as I undid the towel. And there I laid open as pretty a sight as one could wish to see—thirty watches, white and yellow, just lovely to behold.

"Are you a wizard, Mr M'Levy?" said the woman, as she held out her hands; "all that in my house, and me as ignorant of it as a sucking child!"

"I don't doubt you, Mrs Walker," said I; "but confess that you think I should be content."

"Content!" replied she; "I know not what would content you if these didn't. Just offer them to me, and see whether or not I would be content."

"But I am not content," said I; "I want one more."

"Well, I aye thought you were a reasonable man, Mr M'Levy."

"'A ᴡᴀɴᴛ sᴘᴏɪʟs ᴘᴇʀғᴇᴄᴛɪᴏɴ,' Mrs Walker," said I; "and I will not be satisfied till I get this want supplied."

Rolling up my watches I left the house, and went direct to the Office. Mr Moxey was busy with his letters.

"What?" said he, there again, James! I thought you had gone to bed."

"I have just something to do first," said I, as I laid down the parcel, (retaining the bundle of hay.) "Mrs Walker, tavern-keeper, Smith's Close, Grassmarket, presents her compliments to Mr Moxey, and begs to send him two dozen and a half of fresh eggs from Arbroath."

"Eggs to me! are you mad?" But beginning to smell, as he suspected, a trick, he opened the towel, and saw before him Mr C——'s thirty watches.

"Where got?" he asked.

"Where, but in Mrs Walker's tavern, where they naturally fell to be."

"And unknown to her?"

"Close up to the wall beneath the bed, and all, like eggs, enclosed in this hay."

"I'll never interfere with your searches again," he added, laughing. "I'll write this moment, and make C—— a happy man."

"Yes," said I; "and tell him, that, though I'm a *safe* enough *man*, I'm not 'a patent safe.'"

"We've got all."

"No, 'A ᴡᴀɴᴛ sᴘᴏɪʟs ᴘᴇʀғᴇᴄᴛɪᴏɴ,'" said I. "There's one awanting, and without that the rest are nothing."

"Mr C—— will scarcely think that," said he, "You have done enough to-day, and I think you had better go to bed."

"No, I must have *that* watch, otherwise I could sleep none."

I then went to the desk, and taking a printed form of one of our complaints, not filled up, and not signed of course, I put it quietly in my pocket, departed, and took my way to the man Hart's once more. I found him in, just preparing to go to bed.

"My last visit, Hart," said I; "I am come once more for the watch you got from the friend of Mitchell."

"I told you before," said he, "that I have no such watch, and never had."

"And I tell you that I have the very best authority for knowing that you have. Now, Hart, I have known you for some time, and would rather save you than banish you, but," pulling out the useless bit of printed paper, "I have no discretion. There are certain people called authorities, you know, and they have long arms. Do you see that paper? Did you ever hear of such a thing as a complaint?"

"Do you mean a warrant of apprehension?" said he.

"Just as you choose to call it," replied I, taking out my handcuffs. "I am sorry for this duty imposed upon me, but either you or I must suffer. You must walk up to the Office, or I must bid farewell to it."

My man got into a pensive mood, and looked on the floor.

The conjurors on the stage do their work with little things, and they deceive the senses; but they don't often touch the heart. I have done some things in my conjuring way with very puny instruments. Yes, the heart is a conjurable commodity, very simple and helpless when operated upon successfully, and I was here trying to vanquish a stronger one than Mrs Donald M'Leod's, by the means of a bit of paper, with a few words of print on it, and a loop of leather. I have sometimes suspected that the world is juggled in a similar way, only the juggle is not very often known. If so, I may be allowed my small devices, especially when used in the cause of what is good and lawful. I wanted only to save another man's watch. A bit of paper not much larger, once saved the lives of more Roman senators than my watches amounted to altogether.

The first sight of my talisman was not enough. Mr Hart was wary. He hesitated, and struggled with himself for a considerable time—not so much, I thought, for the sake of the watch, as from fear that, after all, I would apprehend him.

"You will do *me*," said he, "as you did the Highlander's wife."

"No," replied I, "I will be on honour with you. Look,—you may make sure work,—I'll not take the watch out of your hands till I have burned the warrant."

The promise caught him. He drew on his stockings again,—for he had been preparing for bed,—put on his shoes and hat, and getting a candle, lighted it.

"Wait here," said he, and went out.

I don't like these *leavings*, I have sometimes found no *returns*; so I followed him to the door, and dogged him to the foot of a close not far from his house. He went up till he came to an old thatched byre, to the top of which he got by means of a heap of rubbish. When I saw the candle glimmering on the top of the house, a solitary light amidst the darkness, and all around as still as death, I could not help thinking of the romance that hangs round the secret ways of vice. The cowkeeper, as he fed his charge, never suspected that there was a treasure over crummie's head; no more did the urchins, who rode on the rigging, dream of the presence of so wonderful a thing to them as a gold watch.

All safe, said I to myself, as I saw the light changing its place, and descending. Then it came down the close, and we stood face to face.

"Here it is," said he; "but I tell you once for all, that I am as powerful a man as you, and that"—

"Stop," said I, "no need, my good fellow; give me your candle. There," continued I, as I applied the blank complaint to the flame, and saw it flare up and die away into a black film, "there's your bargain,—now mine."

And I got the watch, and supplied the *want*."

"Good night, my man; you will sleep sounder without the care and fear of this stolen watch than with it."

This bit of sentiment struck him.

"Well, I believe I will," he said, with a little thickening of the windpipe; "I'll have nothing more to do with stolen property. I have never been happy since I got possession of it."

In a short time, I was before Mr Moxey again, whose letters threatened to terminate in night-work.

"Put that to the rest," said I; *"the want is supplied,—*thirty-two and eighteen make up the fifty, I believe."

"You are refined, James," said he; and perhaps he would not have said it if he had known the story of the old complaint, which for the time I kept to myself. Self-love has its weaknesses. If I had told my device, I might have gratified my vanity; but my trick would have become common property, and thereby lost its charm.

After my day's work, I went home, and was soon asleep.

I acquired a little honour in this matter, although I considered it was not much more than apprentice-work.

I had no objection, however, that my brother bluecoats of the bonny toun should see that M'Levy had not lost the keenness of his scent for such secreted articles as those stolen watches; and this shows that we have our little drops of enjoyment amidst our cares and anxieties, ay, and dangers, and, thank God, happiness is a comparative affair. The word "danger" suggests a few words. I have often been asked, "M'Levy, were you never hurt?" My answer being no,—"M'Levy, was you ever afraid?" My answer the same, though I have been amidst glittering knives before now, ay, and fiery eyes, brighter than the knives; but I early saw that a bold front is the best baton. A detective is done the moment his eye quivers or his arm falters. If firm, there is no risk, or if any, it is from the cowards. A brave thief has something like an understanding of the relation he bears to the laws and its officers. He has a part to play, and he plays it with something so much like the honour of the Honeycombs at cards or dice, that it would surprise you. These latter, to be sure, are only sliders too, and the end of their descent is often deeper than that of their humble brethren of the pea and thimble.

I have only to add, that my men were forthwith brought to trial. The real pith of my histories is to me the *end*; yes all their *charm* to me lies in the tail, although others, and you may readily guess who they are, may think that the the *sting* lies there. I would not, however, give the fact that Clerk got his seven years, and Mitchell his eighteen months as a resetter, for all the *eclat* accorded to any ingenuity I had displayed in bringing about these happy consummations.

The Breathing

❖

One night in 1832, I was at the station in Adam Street, at that time a very disreputable part of the town—it is better now—in consequence of the many bad houses and whisky-shops in the vicinity. There were often rows there, chiefly occasioned by the students, many of whom lodged in the neighbouring streets, so that when our men were called upon it was generally to quell a quarrel, or carry off some poor degraded wretch of a woman for some drunken violence or pocket-picking. On the occasion to which I now allude the call upon us was different. The time was late,—past twelve, and the streets were being resigned to the street-walkers and collegians. All of a sudden a shrill scream of a woman's voice reached my ear, and, running out, I heard a cry that a man of the name of M'—ie, who lived in Adam Street, had been robbed, or attempted to be robbed, on his own stair. Then there was a shout, and a pointing by two or three people,—"They are down to the Pleasance." On such an occasion it has always been my habit not to take up any time by questions for an account of external appearances, because the answers are tedious, and there is more to be gained by time in a rush in the proper direction, trusting to what I may all "criminal indications", than by ascertaining what kind of a coat or hat a man wore, or the length of his nose, or height of body, and so forth. So I noted the index, and took to my toe-points as fast as I could run, down in the direction indicated, but as lightly as I could, for fear of my tread being carried in the silence of the night on to the ears of the runaways. I may mention, too, that I stopped several sympathisers, who were inclined to join, but who, I knew, would only scare, and do no good.

I had the pursuit, if such it may be termed, all to myself, but was immediately "called up" by one of those rock-ahead incidents which are so tantalising to our class,—no other than two roads, each holding out its recommendations to me, the one that the robbers would certainly take to the deep haunts of the Old Town, where the fox-burrows are so inviting and the difficulty of unearthing not easily surmounted; and the other, that they would seek the outskirts, and so get down to the valley between the Pleasance and Arthur Seat, where they might skulk in the deep darkness of the night, and so escape. A minute or two would turn the scale, and I must decide even almost as I ran. I have often quivered in this dilemma, and seldom been wrong in my choice; yet I can't account for one out of ten of these instantaneous decisions. I really believe I have often been swayed by some very trivial incident, perhaps the shuffle of a foot, perhaps a gust of wind not heard as such, but simply as something working upon the ear. The barking of a dog has resolved me, the shutting of a door, or even a greater silence in one direction than another,—nay, to be very plain, and perhaps weak, I have sometimes thought I was led by a superior hand, so directly have I been taken to my quarry. It was so now. It was just as likely the fellows would go north to the Old Town, or south to the Gibbet Toll,—no gibbet now to scare them. I turned to the left down the Pleasance; even as I ran, and about halfway between my turn and Mr Ritchie's brewery, I met one of our men on his beat, coming south, pacing as quietly as if no robbery could have been suspected in his well-watched quarter.

"Met two fellows in a skulk or a run?"

"No one; but before I crossed the foot of Drummond Street, I thought I heard the sound of quick feet, but it stopped in an instant, and I then thought I might have been mistaken."

"Then stand you there as steady as a post, but not as deaf. Keep your feet steady, and your ears open."

I had got just a sniff, and it is not often I have needed more. They had, no doubt, gone that way, and, on observing the officer, had gone into a burrow. I stood for an instant,—no common-stairs here, no closes, no *cul-de-sac*, no hole even for the shrinking body of a robber. The first glance brought me near my wit's end, but not altogether. I have always been led on by small glimpses of Hope's lamp till I got nearer and nearer her temple, and never yet gave up till all was dark. I stepped to the other side of the street, where there are some bad houses. No door open, every window shut, and no light within that could be observed. I could walk with the lightest of feet, and proceeded noiselessly along the narrow pavement till I came to Drummond Street, where there is the recess in which the well stands. I had no hope from that recess because it is comparatively open, and, dark as the night was, they could scarcely have skulked there without the man on the beat seeing them. Yet I was satisfied also that they could not have gone up by Drummond Street. I may mention that I could hear when almost every other person could discover nothing but silence; nay, this quickness of the hearing sense has often been a pain to me, for the tirl of a mouse has often put me off my rest when I stood in great need of it. I require to say nothing of my other poor senses here; they were not needed, for there was nothing to be seen except below the straggling lamps, in the pale light of one of which I saw my man standing sentry, but nothing more.

Expecting nothing from the recess, I crossed to the angle, rather disappointed, and was rather meditative than listening, foiled than hopeful, when my ear was arrested by one or two deep breathings,—scared robbers are great breathers, especially after a tussle with a victim. I could almost tell the kind of play of lungs; it speaks fear, for there is an attempt to repress the sound, and yet nature here cannot be overcome. On the instant I felt sure of my prey, yet I tested my evidence even deliberately. There was more than one play of lungs at work—I could trace two,—and all their efforts, for they had seen the man pass, and had probably heard our conversation, were not able to overcome the proof that was rushing out of their noses, (as if this organ could give out evidence as well as take it in,) not their mouths,—fear shuts the latter, if wonder should open it,—to reach my ear, just as if some great power adopted this mode of showing man that there is a speaking silence that betrays the breakers of God's laws. Now certain I hastened over to the man on the beat, and, whispering to him to go to the station for another man, took my watch again. I knew I had them in my power, because if they took themselves to flight, I could beat them at that trick; so I cooled myself down to patience, and kept my place without moving an inch, quite contented so long as I heard the still half-suppressed respirations.

In a few minutes my men were up, coming rather roughly for such fine work. I took each by the coat-neck,—

"Steady, and not a whisper! They are round the corner,—batons ready, and a rush."

By a combined movement, we all wheeled round the angle, and before another breath could force itself, we had the two chevaliers in our hands,—even as they were standing, bolt upright against the gable of the house that forms one side of the recess. Like all the rest of their craft they were quite innocent, only their oaths—for they were a pair of desperate thimblers, whom I knew at once— might have been sufficient to have modified the effects of their protestations. They were, indeed, dangerous men. They had nearly throttled M'—ie, and in revenge for getting nothing off him had threatened to murder him. My next object was to get them identified by the people who had raised the cry, for if they had dispersed we might have been—with nothing on them belonging to the man— in want of evidence, though not in want of a justification, of our capture of two well-known personages. Fortunately, when we got to the station some of the women were there who identified them on the instant, whereupon they became, as sometimes the very worst of them do, "gentle lambs", and were led very quietly to their destination in the High Street. Remitted to the Sheriff, their doom was fourteen years.

"And the breath of their nostrils shall find them out."

The
Child-
Strippers

❖

How different are the estimates people form of mankind!
Some say that the world is just very much as you take it—
the old notion that truth is just as you think it. If you wear
a rough glove, you may think all those you shake hands with are
rough in the palms; and if you wear a soft one, so in the other way;
and no doubt if you grin in a glass, you will get a grin in return—if
you smile, you will be repaid with a smile. All very well this in the
clever way; but I've a notion that there are depths of depravity not
to be gauged in this short plumb way, just as there are heights of
perfection not to be got at by our own estimates of ourselves. As for
the general "top-to-toe rottenness" so congenial to some religious
sects, why there's a little truth there too—at least I would look
sharp at a man who could turn his eye in and about his own heart,
and just say, with a nice smirk, "Well, I am glad to find that man is
an angel after all." It is as well for me anyhow that I am not given to
making a kaleidoscope of my heart, turning up only varieties of
beauty, without considering that a few hard pebbles form the ele-
ments of the fine display, otherwise how could I have had any belief in the existence of such beings as Kate Lang and Nell Duff. I
would as readily have believed in M. Chaillu's account of the
Gorillas; only these optimist gentry do admit, with a smile of satisfaction, that a hungry tiger is not to be trusted with a live infant—
no more is Kate Lang, say I.

The practice of child-stripping, which is not so common now, is
one of those depths of depravity to which I have alluded. It is not
that there is so much cruelty done. It forms a fine subject for very
tender people who wail about the poor innocents left shivering in

their shirts. But there is more fancy than fact here; they don't shiver long in a crowded city; nay, the stripping is sometimes productive of good, in so much as the neighbours contrive to get the victim pretty well supplied with even better clothes than those stolen. There is more sympathy due to the case which happens sometimes where a heartless thief makes off with the clothes, shirt and all, of a bather, about the solitary parts of Granton; for here the situation of the victim is really terrible. To run after the thief is nearly out of the question as regards success, even if he could make up his mind to a chase in his very *natural* condition; nor is his remaining remedy much better—a walk so unlike that of Adam through Paradise to the nearest house, a mile off, where he must knock at a door, drive away the opener with a scream, bolt like a robber into a bed-room, and get a walk home in a suit of clothes in which his friends cannot recognise him. Our feelings depend often upon such strange turns of thought, that a case of this latter kind, so replete with even agony, can scarcely be told without something like a smile working among the gravely-disposed muscles of the face of the hearer; while that of the child, almost always left its *skin* linen, is viewed with indignation and pity. I cannot explain this difference; but it is not difficult to see how, independently of the rather exaggerated notions we entertain of the condition of the victim, the crime of child-stripping should be visited with the execration it generally meets.

In 1838, and thereabouts, this offence of child-stripping increased to an extent which roused the fears of mothers. The depredators were of course women. My only doubts were, whether there were more than one; for, as I have taken occasion to remark, all such peculiar and out of the way offences are generally the work of some one ingenious artiste; and if more are concerned, they are only parties to a league in which the inventor is the leader. I confess I was more inclined to believe in the single performer, but I was destined in this instance to find myself wrong. I was at least determined to get at the bottom of the mystery, and it wasn't long until I was gratified. In the month of May of the year mentioned, the cases had accumulated, and as yet my inquiries had been unsuccessful. In the New Town the cases had been limited to the narrow streets, and latterly they had increased about the foot of the Canongate. In that quarter, accordingly, I found it necessary to be, though not very expedient to be seen, and I soon got upon my proper scent. One day I observed coming from the Watergate three or four women, all of the lowest section of Conglomerates—not altogether a perfectly applicable name here, in so much as my "clear grits" were not rounded by healthy washings, but sharpened by the abrasion of vice and misery. They were busy tying up a bundle, and after indulging in many stealthy looks to the right and left, they made forward up the Canongate. I might safely have stopped them and made inquiry into the contents of their bundle, but I had something else in view, and was content with noting them, all known to me as they were—cast-off Fancies, not genteel enough for being leagued with respectable thieves, and yet below the summer heat of love—trulls or trollops—trogganmongers during day, and troglodytes during night.

I have said I had hopes, and accordingly I had scarcely lost sight of them when I encountered, a little on this side of the Abbey strand, a small Cupid of a fellow standing in the middle of the street, (he had crept from a stair foot,) having a little bit of a shirt on him coming down to his knees, and crying lustily with beslubbered face.

That's my robbed traveller, said I to myself, as I made up to the young sufferer who had so early fallen among thieves.

And just at the same time as the wondering women of the Watergate were pouring in to see the interesting personage, up comes the mother, who (as I afterwards learned) having sent out Johnny for a loaf of bread, and finding he didn't return, issued forth to seek for him. One may guess her astonishment at meeting him within so short a time, probably not ten minutes, in a state approaching to nudity, but the guess would hardly come up to the real thing. The notion of his having been robbed and stripped didn't occur to her, and her amazement did not abate until I told her the truth, whereupon the women—like so many hens whose chickens had been seized by a hawk—broke into a scream of execration which excited the wit of an Irishman, "Have the vagabonds taken the watch from the gintleman? Why didn't they take the shirt too, and make a naked shaim ov it?" And having taken the name of the mother, I made after my strippers.

Nor was it long until I got them again within my vision. It seemed to be a feasting-day with the ogresses. They met and parted, every one looking out for some little Red Riding-hood, who was doubt-less unconscious of the tender mercies of the she-wolves. The league consisted of five, all of whom had been through my hands for thefts and robberies—Catharine Lang, Helen Duff, Mary Joice, Margaret Joice, and Robina Finnie. If you have ever been among the wynds, you can form an idea of these hags; if you haven't, you must excuse me—squalor-painting is at best a mud-daub. Amongst all, mark this strange feature—that though some of them had been mothers, the mother was here inverted, the natural feelings turned upside down; the innocent creatures for whom some stray sympathy might have been expected, changed into objects of rapine and cruelty for the sake of a few rags. I soon not only marked their movements, but saw that an opportunity waited them—for where in the Old Town will you not find clots of children? and are not these, when engaged in play, artless and confiding? Who, however degraded, will harm them? Nay, if there is any creature secure from the drunkard, the libertine, or the thief, it is the merry playmates of the pavement, whose gambols bring back to the seared heart of the vicious the happiness and innocence they have so long been strangers to. Yes, all true, though a little poetical; but I suspect there is a depth even *below* vice.

The wolves' eyes were, as I could see, on the merry Red Riding-hoods; and as their number was five, I beckoned to a constable to get one or two of his brethren and watch in the neighbouring close-mouths. As for myself, I betook me to a stair-foot at the top of New Street, where, besides the advantage of a look-out, I had the chance, according to my calculation, of being on the very spot of the ex-pected operation, for there were but few convenient places about. The women were so intent upon their victims, that they seemed to

have forgotten that while they were supervising they might themselves be supervised. Nor was it long before I began to see that my
expectations would be realised. Lang had almost immediately the
best dressed of the gambolers in her *motherly* hand, and the bit of
sugar-candy was working its charm; so true it is that there is await-
ing every one a bait at the end of the standing line, stretched out in
the waters of life, about which we are always swimming and flap-
ping our tails, passing and repassing without ever dreaming of the
hook. Ay, there are big fish intent upon large enterprises among the
deeper places, who will snap at the dead worm even in the midst of
living gold-fish. And is it not a pleasure sometimes to see them
caught by the garbage when one can net the angler as well as the
angled? My moral applies not to the gudgeons, but the pikes.

Yes, I was right; Lang, with the girl in her hand, and followed by
Duff and one of the Joices, made right for my entry. I stepped up
the stair a few paces to be out of the way. I wanted for ardent reasons that the operation should be as complete as possible, for the
cancer had become too deep for any good from mere skin-cutting.
The moment they got the confiding soul in, who no doubt thought
herself in hands far more kindly than her mother's, the sugar-candy
of temptation was changed for the aloes of force. The three, stimu-
lated by the fear of some one coming in upon them, either from
below or above, flew at her like hawks pouncing upon a gowdie.
Did ever before the fingers of ogresses go with such rapidity to strip
the clothes that they might gobble up the body? The little mouth,
still stuffed with the sweet bait, was taken care of by a rough hand.
The plucking was the work of an instant—bonnet, pinny, napkin,
frock, petticoats, boots and stockings.

"It's a good shurt, Kate."

"Worth a shilling, Nell."

"Off wid it," cried Joice.

The little chemise is whirled over the head, and the minum
"nude" is left roaring alone—a chance living lay figure, which would
have charmed even Lord Haddo, if he had a palette and brush,
with its exquisite natural tints.

If I had had time to wait and see, I might have observed a bit of child life also worthy of a Paton or a Faed; for just as I was hurrying down, in came rushing the playmates, all with wondering eyes to see Phemy (I ascertained her name afterwards) standing naked within a few minutes after she had left their play. Do you think they would ever forget that sight all their born days? But I had another sight in view more interesting to me—even one in wolf-life, with some difference in expression and tints—the grandmammas with the canines and long claws, so formidable to the Riding-hoods. Nor was I disappointed. I had set my trap so well that I had no need of the candy-bait. The instant the constables had seen what was going on, they had laid hold of the other Joice and Robina Finnie, and the three who had been engaged, having seen their dear sisters in custody, turned down New Street, up which they had gone a few steps, and were seized by me and another constable from behind. Meanwhile the cries of the little nude, mixed with those of her tiny sisterhood, brought a crowd, who, instantly ascertaining the cause of all the uproar, showered their indignation on the culprits with a severity that excluded even Irish humour. Nay, so furious were the hen-mothers, that unless we had taken good care of our sparrow-hawks, there would that day have been more stript than Phemy and her brother-victim of the Watergate; nor would I have answered for discolorations or broken bones. But care was also taken of the tender chicken, who, rolled up in a shawl, became in the midst of the crowd a little heroine, honoured with more endearing epithets and sympathetic condolences than would perhaps ever fall to her portion again.

At the top of the street we collected our prisoners, and marched them gallantly up the Canongate and High Street. One likes to possess the favour of the female part of the people, and this day I got as much of the incense of hero-worship as if I had stopped a massacre of the innocents. I am not sure if some males, too, much given to baby-love, did not glugger with reddened gills in anger at the spoilers of their wives' darlings; all which was no doubt heightened by the impression then in the public mind, produced by the repeated accounts of the instances of this nefarious traffic. The prisoners had even during the previous part of that day committed four strippings of the same kind besides those I had witnessed.

It was not long till I ascertained that I had been wrong in my original conjecture, and that the whole of these thefts had been perpetrated by a gang. During their confinement, and when we expected that they would hold out in their denial of guilt, it was quite a scene to witness the identifications. The witnesses were, of course, the little victims themselves, on whose minds the features of the women had been so indelibly impressed, especially where, like the case of Phemy, "the shurt was a good un," that they not only knew them, but screamed with terror the moment they were brought before them. And to the women, no doubt, they were of that kind of terrible infants so well described by the French, the more by reason, perhaps, that among that people the children have more strange things to see than in our decent country. From searches we got the evidence of the little wardrobes themselves, chiefly through pawns, showing the immense extent of their assiduous labours. Nor had it been an unprofitable traffic to them; many of the dresses were taken from well-dressed youngsters in the New Town, and you have only to buy those things to know what money it costs to rigg out a little man or woman in our day, when the children are taught pride and a love of finery with the supping of porridge. But, after all, it came out that we didn't need these evidences. The vagabonds broke down in the end under the accumulation of proof, and admitted to I do not know how many strippings. They each got eighteen months' imprisonment, and the community was relieved from the cold-blooded and unfeeling practice of child-stripping for a long period afterwards.

The
White
Coffin

❖

If the Conglomerates of our Old Town are troubled with many miseries, as the consequences of their privations and vices, it is certain the whole squalid theatre they play their strange parts in, is the scene of more incidents, often humorous, nay romantic—if there can be a romance of low life—than can be found in the quiet saloons of the higher grades in the New Town. The observation indeed is almost so trite, that I need not mention that while in the one case you have nature over-laid with the art of concealment, the slave of decorum, in the other you have the old mother, free, fresh, and frisky—her true characters, rapid movements, quiet thoughts, intertwined plots, the jerks of passion, the humorous and the serious, the comedy and the melodrama of the tale of life—an idiot's one, if you please, even in the grave ranks of the highest.

In February 1837, as I was on my saunter with my faithful Mulholland among the haunts of the Old Town, we observed our old friends Andrew Ireland, John Templeton, and David Toppen, doubling the mouth of one of the closes leading to Paul's Work. These industrious gentry are never idle; as they carry their tools along with them, they can work anywhere; and, like the authors, a species of vagabonds who live on their wits, and steal one from another, they need no stock in trade. It was clear to me that we were unobserved, and proceeding down another close, I expected to meet them probably about their scene of action. I may mention that I was somewhat quickened in my movements by some recollections that Ireland had cost me a deal of trouble—the more by token that he was called "the Climber", as being the best hand at a scramble, when cats would shudder, in all the city, for which he had refused for sometime to give me even the pledge of his body. We got down the close and round the corner, just in the nick of time to see the tail of Andrew's coat disappearing from the top of a pretty high dyke. The two others followed the example of the Climber, and when they had disappeared, we placed ourselves at the side of the wall to receive them on their descent. The cackling of fowls soon told us the nature of their work, and the gluggering of choking craigs was a clear indication that the robbers were acting on the old rule that "the dead tell no tales."

"Sure of the Climber this time," I said to my assistant. "I will seize Andrew and Templeton, and lay you hold of Toppen."

And the words were scarcely out of my mouth, when we received gratefully our friends in our arms. The dead hens were flung away, and darting at the throats of my two charges, I secured them on the instant. Mulholland lost his hold, but so pleased was I at my capture, especially of Andrew, that I could not resist a few words in my old way.

"I was afraid you would fall and break your neck, Andrew," said I.

"Thank you for the warm reception," replied the cool rogue, as he recovered breath after the short tussle.

"No apology," said I. "I have told you by a hundred looks that I wanted you."

"And sold for a hen at last," he added, with an oath.

"And not allowed to eat it," said I. "What a glorious supper you and the old woman would have had!"

The taunt was at least due to his oath.

"Pick up the hens, Mulholland," said I, "and let us march, we will have a laugh in the High Street."

And proceeding with my man in each hand till I came to the head of the close, I gave one of them in charge of a constable, retaining the other. Mulholland with the hens brought up the rear, and I believe we cut a good figure in our march, if I could judge from the shouts of the urchins—tickled with a kind of walking anecdote, that carried its meaning so clearly in the face of it, for it is seldom that the booty makes its appearance in these processions.

On arriving at the Office, my charges were locked up. Toppen was caught the same evening; and this part of my story of the metamorphosis being so far preclusive, I may just say that my hen-stealers were forthwith tried by the Sheriff and a jury. Each got the price of his hen even at a higher rate than the present price of a fashionable cockerel—Ireland getting nine months, Templeton six, and Toppen four. But the Climber vindicated his great reputation in a manner that entitled him to still greater fame. Whether it was that the jailer was not made aware of his abilities, or that he was placed in a cell which it was held to be impossible for any creature without claws on all the four members to get out of, I cannot say; but true it is that, to the utter amazement of every one connected with the jail, Andrew Ireland got out by the skylight, and finding his way over ridges and down descents that might have defied an Orkney eagle-hunter, descended at the north back of the Canongate, and got clear off.

Once more "done" by my agile friend, my pride was up, and I must have him by hook or by crook. I knew he was one of those enchanted beings whose love to the Old Town prevents them from leaving it. It has such a charm for them that they will stick to it at all hazards, even when, day by day, and night by night, they are hounded through closes and alleys like wild beasts, and have, as it were, nowhere to lay their heads. I have known them sleep on the tops of houses, and in crannies of old buildings, half-starved and half-clothed, in all weathers, summer or winter, rather than seek rest by leaving the scenes of their wild infancy. And all this they will do in the almost dead certainty that ultimately they will be seized. I was thus satisfied that Andrew was about the town; and even when, after the lapse of months, I could get no trace of him, I still retained my conviction that he was in hiding.

That conviction was destined to receive a grotesque and grim verification. I was one day at the top of Leith Wynd. A number of people were looking at the slow march of some poor wretch's funeral, the coffin borne by some ragged Irishmen, a few others going behind. As I stood looking at the solemn affair—more solemn and impressive to right minds than the plumed pageant that leaves the mansion with the inverted shield, and goes to the vault where are conserved, with the care of sacred relics, the remains of proud ancestors—a poor woman, who seemed to have been among the mourners, came up to me.

"And do you see your work, now?" quoth she, in a true Irish accent. "Do you know who is in that white coffin there, wid the bit black cloth over it?"

"No," said I.

"And you don't know the darling you murthered for stealing a hen at Paul's Work?"

"You don't mean to say," replied I, "that that's the funeral of your son, Mrs Ireland?"

"Ay, and, by my soul, I do, and murthered by you. He never lifted up his head agin, but pined and dwined like a heart-broken cratur as he was; and now he's there going as fast as the boys can carry him to his grave."

"Well," said I, "I am sorry for it."

"The devil a bit of you, you vagabond! It's all sham and blarney, and a burning shame to you, to boot."

"Peace, Janet," said I; "he's perhaps happier now than he was here stealing and drinking. There are no sky-lights in the Canongate graves, and he'll not climb out to do any more evil."

"Sky-lights!" cried Janet; "ay, but there is, and Andrew Ireland will climb out and get to heaven, while you, you varmint, will be breaking firewood in h— to roast their honours the judges who condemned my innocent darling."

"Quiet, Janet."

"Well, thin, to roast yourself; will that plaise ye?"

"Yes, yes," said I.

And fearing the woman's passions, inflamed by her grief, might reach the height of a howl, I moved away, while she, muttering words of wrath, proceeded after the white coffin. Nor can I say I was altogether comfortable as I proceeded to the Office, for there is something in the wild, moving yet miserable lives of these Arabs of the wynds when wound up by death that is really touching. Nay, it is scarcely possible to avoid the thought that they are not free agents, if they do not claim from our sympathy the character of victims. In truth I was getting muffish, if I did not soliloquise a bit about other climbers whose feet rested on the backs of such poor wretches, and who, by means not very different, get into high places, where they join the fashionable cry about philanthropy—yes, a philanthropy that helps the devil, by allowing him to brain the objects they attempt to benefit.

But a police-office soon takes the softness out of a man. I had scarcely entered when I got notice of a robbery, committed on the prior night at the workshop of Messrs Robb and Whittens, working silversmiths in Thistle Street. On repairing to the spot, I ascertained that the robber had made off with a number of silver articles, sugar-tongs, spoons, and other valuables; among the rest a number of silver screws. I particularly notice these, because they served my purpose in quite another way than that for which they were originally intended. But as to the manner of the robbery, I could get no satisfactory information beyond the fact that a suspicion attached to two chimney-sweeps, who had been passing in the morning, and had been employed to sweep the vents of the workshop; nor was my disappointment lessened by finding that the sweeps were utterly unknown to the parties connected with the shop. They could not even tell whether they came from the New Town or the Old. Then as to identification, even had I been angel enough to bring so unrecognisable a creature before them, who ever heard of any distinctive features in a chimney-sweep, if he has not a hump on his back or wants a nose on his face! Even I, who have seen through all manner of disguises, am often at fault with them until I almost rub noses with them—a process in which I would catch a "devilish sight" more than I wanted.

Notwithstanding these difficulties, I did not altogether despair, insomuch as I at least became pretty well satisfied that it really was the gentlemen in black who had done the deed. So wherever there was smoke to be cured and vents swept, I considered it my duty

to call and try if I could find, not the features of my men, but some
trace of the tongs and screws; for in many cases where I have had
right to search, I have got my pipe lighted at a fire, the light of
which has shown me what I wanted. Yet all wouldn't do; nor was I a
whit more lucky among the brokers and pawn-shops. Nay, although
I *screwed* my ingenuity to the last turn, could I trace anything of
the stolen silver screws. It was no go, as the lovers of slang say; and
if it had not been that I was born never to know the meaning of
"Give it up," I would have renounced the pursuit of men who are
beyond the landmarks of society.

Not altogether without a result, however, these vain searches. I
was impressed with a curiosity about chimney-sweeps, and I never
eyed one without a wish to know something about him. They had
formerly interested me very little; for, to do them justice, though
they have means of entering houses seldom in the power of others,
and which none but fiery lovers ever think of, they have seldom
qualified themselves for my attentions. They have no likings for
the whitewashing processes of jails. At the same time, however, as
cleanliness is next to godliness, they seldom appear in church; the
grace would not pay the soap.

With this affection for the tribe still hanging about me, I was
one day, a considerable period after the robbery, going along the
Pleasance, in an expedition connected with the house called the
Castle of Clouts, where I expected to find some remnants not left by
the builder of that famous pile. I was not looking for sweeps, and
yet my pipe was not out. I had been blowing some puffs, when, on
turning round, I saw two of my black gentlemen standing smoking
loungingly, with their backs to the wall. "Ah, some of the bright
creatures of my fancy," thought I; "yea, those aerial beings who for
months have been hovering over me in my dreams, yet altogether
without wings." My first act was to put that same pipe out, my next
to watch their movements. They were very busy talking to each
other; but what interested me most was the curiosity with which
they were contemplating some articles which one of them was
showing to the other,—nay, there seemed to be a silvery look about

the things, which was the more apparent that they were a contrast to the hands that held them.

So straightway my pipe, which I had extinguished, required a light, and these curers of smoke could even produce that which they professed to banish. In a moment I was standing before them.

"Well, lads," said I, "can you give me a light?"

One of them recoiled a little as he caught my eye. He seemed to know me, though I am free to confess I did not know him.

"To be sure," said the other.

And striking a match upon the wall he handed me a light, where-upon I began to puff away; and as smoking is a social act, I found myself irresistibly attracted by my friend, who in my first going up appeared to be so shy.

"Do you know where the Castle of Clouts is?" said I, as I peered and peered into the dark face of him who tried to avoid my gaze.

But I was still at fault. His features were familiar to me, but the soot still came between me and my identification. At length I got my clue.

"Andrew Ireland," said I, "when did you come out of the Canongate churchyard? Was there a skylight in the top of the coffin?"

"Andrew Stewart is my name," replied the black ghost.

"And when did you turn sweep, Andrew?"

"When seven years old," said he; "but I tell you my name is Stewart, and be d——d to you."

"Well, I don't apprehend names," said I, "only bodies. Then I'm not sure if you are not a spirit, for Janet showed me your coffin on its way to the Canongate."

"Perhaps it was Andrew Ireland's coffin you saw," said he. "It wasn't mine, anyhow."

"Oh, I see," said I, "it would be Andrew Stewart's, and I have committed a mistake. No matter; I want to know what you have in your right coat-pocket."

And at the same instant I held up my hand. My assistant was presently at my side. I saw by the fire of his eye—something like a chimney on fire—that he was bent on resistance, and instantly taking him by the neckcloth with my right hand, I was proceeding to plunge my left into his pocket, when he seized me with his wonted ferocity, and for his pains got himself laid on his back.

"Now, Andrew," said I, as he lay grinning at me so like another black gentleman when angry, "as sure as you are your mother's darling, I will take you up and throw you again if you are not peaceable, and behave yourself like a gentleman."

And getting my assistant to hold him, I took from his pocket three silver screws. It was all up with my ghost, who almost instantly became as gentle as these creatures, even the real white kind, generally are. He got up, and we proceeded to the Office. Nor did all the parts of this remarkable case end here, for, as we passed along St Mary's Wynd, whom should we meet but Janet Ireland. The moment she saw us, she appeared stupified.

"He is risen again, Janet," said I, in a kind of whisper, "they forgot to fasten the coffin with the silver screws."

"And the more shame yours, you thaif of a thousand," she cried, "to steal the darling boy of a poor widow. Dead! Isn't he worse than dead when in the hands of the biggest scoundrel that ever walked the airth?"

And what, in addition to this ingenuous turn which Janet gave to the story of the white coffin, Janet said or roared, I cannot tell, for we hurried away to avoid a gathering crowd.

I will never forget the look of the Superintendent when I told him that the man before him was the dead and buried Andrew Ireland, the stealer of the hens, the climber through the skylight of the jail, and the robber of the silversmiths shop. What puzzled him most was, how, with the conviction on my mind that the lad was dead and buried, I could have recognised him through the soot. He looked at him again and again, nor could he say that, with the minutest investigation, he could say that he recognised the well-known thief who had cost us so much trouble.

Andrew was tried for the escape from prison as well as for the robbery; and that the judges did not think he was the short-lived person described by Janet, appears from the judgment, which condemned him to fourteen years' transportation.

The
Cobbler's
Knife

❖

Y ou will have perceived that among my mysteries I have never had anything to do with dreams or dream-mongers. My dreams have been all of that peep-o'-day kind when a man is "wide awake" as they say, and "up to a thing or two". Not to say that I disbelieve in dreams when they have a streak of sunlight in them, as all veritable ones have. Nor is the strange case I am about to relate free from the suspicion that the dream which preceded a terrible act, was just a daylight feeling reflected from some dark corner of the brain.

In 1835, I met one morning, as I was going to commence the duties of the day, William Wright, shoemaker in Fountain Close. He had been drinking the evening before, for his eyes were red and swollen, and he had the twittering about the tumified top of the cheeks, which shows that the inflammation is getting vent. There was some wildness in his look, and, as it afterwards appeared, something in his talk with a deeper meaning than I could comprehend.

"You have had more than enough last night, William," said I.

"Why, yes," replied he, "James and I had a bout, and I am off work for an hour or two till my hand steadies."

"Better for you and your wife if your hand was always steady," said I, as I made a movement to walk on.

"Do you believe in dreams?"

"Some," replied I, meaning the streaked ones I have alluded to. "Why do you put that question?"

"Because," replied he, "I am quite disturbed this morning by one I had last night. I thought that James Imrie stabbed me with the knife I cut my leather with."

"But James hasn't done it yet, has he?"

"No, but I awoke as angry at him as if he had; and though I have come out to get a mouthful of fresh air, I can't get quit of my wrath."

"Angry at a dream," said I, as I looked into William's scowling face. "I thought we had all quite enough to be angry at, without having recourse to dreams."

"Ay, but I can't help it," said he again; "I have been trying to shake it off, but it won't do."

"It will fly off with the whisky fever, William," said I. "James and you are old friends, and you mustn't allow a dream to break your friendship."

"Wouldn't like that either," was the reply. "He's a good-natured creature, and I like him; but I can't get quit of his visage as he stuck the knife into me. It has haunted me all the morning."

"So that you would reverse the dream, and make it true by *contraries*, as the old ladies do, when they can't get things to fit— by sticking the knife into *him*?"

"No, I wouldn't feel it in my heart to stab the best friend I have," said he; and looking wistfully into my face with his bloodshot eyes, he added, "But maybe a glass with James will wear it off."

"Yes, of pure spring water from the Fountain well there," said I.

"I never was very fond of water," said he, with a kind of grim smile, "nor is it very fond of me. One can't talk over it."

"Your old political twists, William," said I, as I recollected a curious theory he sported everywhere, and was rather mad upon.

"Oh, but I don't hate James for opposing me in that. I rather like him the better for it. We get fun out of it."

"The more reason," said I, "for you to give up your ill-natured fancy. Stab you!—why, man, James Imrie is so inoffensive a creature, that, though a flesher's runner, he wouldn't flap a fly that blows his beef, unless it were a very tempting bluebottle."

"I believe it," said he, looking a little more calm; "and I will try to forget the face. I will be better after my breakfast."

So I left William to his morning meal, suspecting that there would be a dram before it, thinking too of the strange fancy that had taken possession of him, but never dreaming that anything would come of it. It was some time afterwards that the thread of the story again recurred to my mind, and what I have now to relate was derived from a conversation I had with Wright himself at a time when he was likely to speak the truth. I cannot answer for every word of the conversation I am to report, but I have little doubt that the substance comes as near the thing as other recitals of the same kind recorded a considerable time after they have occurred.

It appeared that James Imrie, according to his old habit, and without knowing anything of William's dream, had left his house in Skinner's Close, and gone to his friend's, for the purpose of having a crack and a spark. William, who was at the time busy with a job of cobbling which he had promised to finish that night, received his friend with all his usual warmth, but, what was strange enough, without saying a word of his dream. James sat at a little side-table near William's stool, and some whisky was produced, according to their old fashion; for the shoemaker, like other political cobblers, liked nothing better than to spin his politics and take his dram while he was plying his awl and rosin-end. So scarcely had the first glass been swallowed, when William got upon his hobby—"The five acres and the thousand pounds" doctrine as he used to call it, and which the reader will understand as the conversation progresses. Poor James was no great adept at the sublime mystery that, like Fourier's, was to regenerate the world, and make every snob and flesher's runner as happy as the denizens of Paradise; and therefore, with his tardy thoughts and slow Scotch pronunciation, was no match for his book-read and voluble antagonist; but he was a good "butt", and that was all probably that Wright cared for—his sole ambition being to speak and to be heard speaking by any one, however unable to understand the extent of his learning.

"There now," began William, "I have been reading in the *Scotsman* to-day that the Duke of Buccleuch has a thousand a-day. Good Lord! just think, if all the land possessed by this one man, made of clay no finer than the potter's, and maybe not so well turned, was divided into ploughgates, how many poor people would be lairds, and rendered happy."

"But if we were a' lairds," drawled James, "wha wad mak' the shoon and rin wi' the beef?"

"They would make their own shoes out of their own leather, and rear their own beef," was the triumphant reply. "Then, people say I'm for French equality. I'm not. The idiots don't understand the 'five acres and thousand pounds' doctrine. No man should have more than that quality of land, or that sum of money. The overplus should be taken from him and divided."

"It looks weel," replied James, with a good-natured smile; "but how would it work? It puts me in mind o' Laird Gilmour's plan wi' his snuff. 'Let every prudent man ken,' said he, 'that there's twa hundred pinches in half an unce; and let him keep count as he taks every pinch, and his nose will never cheat him, and he'll never cheat his nose.' I've tried it, but I aye lost count."

"Nonsense, man! You're just like the rest, trying to crack a joke at the expense of a grand scheme for benefiting our species. You forget that under our present idiotic system a poor man cannot often get his half ounce to divide into pinches, whereas under the 'five acres and thousand pounds' doctrine you could rear your own to-bacco, dry it, make Taddy of it, and then snuff it, without the necessity of your arithmetic."

"And mak' our ain whisky tae," rejoined James, "and get a' drunk?"

"No," responded the theorist. "We might certainly distil our own whisky, but not get all drunk. Drunkenness is the consequence of our present system, where poverty makes misery, and misery flies to the bottle, and where bloated wealth produces epicures, who disdain whisky, but wallow in wine from morning to night."

"And yet they're no ill chields, thae grand folk, after a'," said James. "Mony a shilling I get when my basket's emptied. It comes a' round. If they get, they gie; and they're no unmindfu' o' the puir."

"I'm poor," cried the cobbler; "do they mind me? No. They grind me down to a farthing, and are ready to say, when I support the rights of labour, 'Well, labour then, and be paid; and when you can't work, you have the workhouse between you and starvation.' And yet I have a soul as noble as theirs."

"And nobler," said James, with his quiet humour; "for you would mak' a paradise o' the world, and every ane o' us an angel without wings; but we wouldna' need wings, for wha would think o' fleeing out o' paradise?"

"Your old mockery, James," said Wright, a little touched. "The great problem of the happiness of mankind is not a subject for ridicule."

"It's yoursel' that's making the fun," rejoined his friend. "I was only using your ain words. But could we no speak about something else than the 'five acres and thousand pounds' doctrine? I never could comprehend it."

"And never can," was the tart reply. "You haven't capacity. It requires deep thought to solve the problem of human happiness, and you needn't try; but you might listen to instruction."

"I have listened lang aneugh," said the other, alike ruffled in his turn, "and it comes aye to the same knotted thrum. Ye canna mak a gude job o't by slicing aff the lords and the puir. Ye might as weel try to fancy a sheep wi' nae mair body than a king's-hood and some trollops, without head or trotters." And James laughed good-naturedly.

"Gibes again," retorted Wright, as (according to his account to me) the vision of the dream came before him, and the anger which had accompanied it flared upon his heart.

But he wrestled with it, occasionally looking at his friend, whom he really loved, yet still fancying that the face of that friend, however illuminated with the good humour probably inspired by the whisky, might or would assume the demoniac expression it carried when he dreamed that he had stabbed him to the heart. It signified little that James was smiling,—the other expression would return when the smile left. It was embodied in the muscles. It appeared as a phantasm, and the strength of a morbid imagination gave it form and expression.

"Yes, the old gibes."

"No," replied James; "I canna jibe wi' an auld freend. But to end a' this just never speak mair o' the new paradise."

"Worse and worse!" cried Wright. "You despise a subject that ought to interest all people. What are you who laugh at the idea of being made a proprietor of the rights of man—a poor wretch, who makes a shilling a-day by carrying beef, and licks the hand that gives you a penny, which by the rights of nature belongs to you; for is it not robbed from you by your masters, who have made a forceful division of property, and then you scoff at the man who would right you. I say, man, you're a born idiot."

A word this that changed James's face into as much of ill-nature as the poor fellow's naturally good and simple heart would permit. Wright at that moment looked at him. He saw, as he thought, the very countenance of the stabber, and his heart burned again, his eye flashed, and he instinctively grasped the knife in his hand. The fit lasted for a moment and went off, and the conversation was renewed at a point where I break off my narrative, to resume it when Wright gave me the parting words.

All this time I was in my own house. It would be, I think, about nine o'clock when I left to go up the High Street. I saw a number of people collected at the mouth of the Fountain Close, and heard dreadful cries of murder from the high windows of a house a little way down the entry. I was not thinking of Wright, and pushing the people aside, I was beginning to make my way down, when up the close comes running a man in his shirt-sleeves. I caught him in an instant in my arms, while the people were crying wildly, the women screaming, "Take care of the knife!"

And to be sure the knife was in his hand, *all bloody.*

"Wright!" cried I, as I wrenched the weapon from him.

"Ay, Wright," replied he; "I have murdered James," and then drawing a deep sigh he added, in choking accents. "Oh, that dream!"

Holding him tight I got him from amongst the crowd for indeed at the time I thought him mad. In leading him up I began to recollect the story he had told me before. I wished to speak, but when I turned to him I beheld such a wild distortion of features that I shrunk from increasing his agony. I heard him groaning, every groan getting into the articulation, "My friend," "My best friend," "Surely I am mad," "Take care of me, M'Levy—I'm a maniac." I didn't think so now, yet I was upon my guard, and, as he was a strong man, I got a constable to take him by the other arm.

On arriving at the Office, which we did in the midst of a dense crowd, among whom the word "murder" sped from mouth to mouth, making open lips and wide staring eyes, I led him in. The moment he entered, he flung himself on a seat, and covering his eyes with his hands sent forth gurgling sounds, as if his chest were convulsed— rolling meanwhile from side to side, striking his head on the back of the seat, and still the words, "James, James, my old friend—O God! what is this I have brought upon me?"

"Is Imrie dead?" said I, watching him narrowly.

"Dead!" he cried, with a kind of wild satire, even light as a madman's laugh; "up to the heft in his bowels."

"Was it connected with the dream, William?" I said again; "why, it was James should have stabbed you."

"The dream," he ejaculated, as if his spirit had retired back into his heart; "the dream—ay, the dream. It was that—it was that."

"How could that be?" I said again, for I was in a difficulty.

"His face, the very face he had when, in my dream, he plunged my own knife in me, has haunted me ever since. I told you that morning it was with me. I could not get rid of it, and when I saw him to-night sitting by me, I observed the same scowl. I thought he was going to seize my knife and stab me. I thought I would prevent him by being before him, and plunged the knife into his body."

"Terrible delusion," said I. "Imrie, as I told you, couldn't have hurt a fly."

"Too late, too late," he groaned. "I know it now, and, what is worst of all, I'm not mad; I feel I am not, and I must be hanged. Nothing else will satisfy my mind—I have said it. If not, I will destroy myself—lend me my knife."

"No, no," said I, "no murders here; but perhaps James is not dead—he may recover."

"Why do you say that?" he cried, as he slipt off the chair, and took me by the knees; "who knows that? has any one seen him to tell you? I would give the world and my existence to know that he has got one remnant of life in him;" and then he added, as his head fell upon his chest, "Alas! it is impossible. I took too good care of that. It would have done for one of his master's oxen."

"Imrie's not dead," said a constable, as he came forward "they've taken him to the Infirmary."

I have seen a criminal with his whole soul in his ear as the jury took their seats, and seen his eye after the transference of his spirit from the one organ to the other, as he heard the words "Not guilty". So appeared Wright. He rose up, and again seating himself, while his eye was still fixed on the bearer of good news, he held up his hands in an attitude of prayer, and kept muttering words which I could not hear.

On leading him to the cell, where he was in solitude to be left for the night, I could not help thinking, as I have done on other occasions, that the first night is the true period of torture to such a one as Wright, with remorse in his heart. I suspect we cannot picture those agonies of the spirit except by some comparisons with our experiences of pain; but as pain changes its character with every pang, as it responds to the ever-coming and varying thoughts, our efforts are simply ineffectual. We give a shudder, and fly to some other thought for relief. To a sufferer such as Wright, we can picture only one alternative—the total renunciation of the spirit to God, and how wonderfully the constitution of the mind is suited to this, the deepest remorse finding the readiest way where we would think it might be reversed. It is impossible to rid one's self of the conviction from this strange fact alone, that Christianity, which harmonises with this instinct, so to call it, comes from the God of the instinct. It seemed to me that Wright would, in the ensuing night, find the solace he seemed to yearn for. He had already got some hope; and becoming calm, I sat down beside him for a short time, for I had known him as a decent, hard-working fellow, incapable, except under some frenzy, of committing murder. I got from him the conversation with Imrie, which I have given partly, I doubt not, in that incorrect way, as to the set form of words, inseparable from such narratives.

"When I called James an idiot," he continued, "I saw the expression, as I thought, coming over his face, and I had the feeling I had in my dream, but I soon saw the old smile there again, and was soon reconciled.

"'Weel, maybe I am an idiot,' said James, 'for I've been aye dangling my bonnet in the presence o' customers, when maybe if I had clapt it on my head wi' a gude thud o' my hand, and said, "I'm as gude as you," and forced my way i' the warld, I wouldna, this day, be ca'd Jamie Imrie, the flesher's porter.'

"And the good soul smiled again, so we took another glass of the whisky,—a good thing when it works in a good heart, but a fearful one when it rouses the latent corruption of a bad one. I fear it wrought so with me, for although we were old friends, I got still moodier, thinking more and more of my dream, while James became more humorous.

"'But, Willie, my dear Willie,' he said, 'idiot as I may be, I doot if I would ha'e been better under your system, for I would hae been a daft laird o' five acres, and gi'en awa' my snuff and my whisky, and maybe my turnips, to my freends, and got in debt and been a bankrupt proprietor; so, just to be plain wi' you, and I've thought o' tellin' ye this afore nou, I would recommend you to gi'e up this new-fangled nonsense o' yours, or rather, I should say, auld-fangled, for you've been at it since ever I mind. Naebody seems to understand it, and here's a bit o' a secret,' lowering his voice, 'the folks lauch at ye when you're walking on the street, and say, "There's the political cobbler that's to cobble up society."'

"'Laugh at me!' I cried, in my roused wrath, yet I had borne ten times more from my old friend; 'laugh at me, you villain!'

"Then James's face grew dark—I watched it, it was the very face of my dream. The drink deceived me, no doubt, but I was certain of what I saw. I observed him move, as if he wanted the knife. Oh, terrible delusion! I believe the good soul had no such intention; but I was carried away by some mysterious agency. I thought I was called upon to defend myself against murder; I grasped the knife, and in an instant plunged it into his belly, and as I drew out the weapon, the blood gushed forth like a well. 'Oh, Willie!' he cried, and fell at my feet.

"I immediately roared for help, and in ran my wife, followed by neighbours. With the knife in my hand, I rushed out, and fell into your arms. Now, can you read this story, and tell me the meaning of it? I have already said I am not mad; but why was I led by a dream to stab my friend? Is there any meaning in my conduct as directed by Providence?"

"I just fear, William," said I, "from what I observed in you that morning when you told me your dream, that you had been drinking too much whisky, which, fevering and distempering your mind, produced not only the dream, but the subsequent notion that poor James was intent upon killing you. You will now see the consequence of drink. One may trace the effects of it for a time, but when, after a certain period, it begins to work changes in the tormented and worried brain, no man can calculate the results, or the crimes to which it may lead."

"I believe you are right," replied he; "and if James would just recover, he would be dearer to me than ever, and whisky no longer a deceitful friend; but, ah! I fear. And then how am I to pass this night in a dark cell, with no one near me, and the vision of that bleeding body before my eyes aye, and those words sounding in my ear, which torture and wring my heart more than a thousand oaths—those simple words, 'Oh, Willie!' "

"You must trust where trust can find a bottom," said I; "perhaps Imrie may live and recover."

"God grant!" groaned the prisoner.

And with a sorrowful heart, I turned the key in the lock.

Next day, it was ascertained that Imrie had passed a night of extreme suffering, and then died. This information I conveyed to

Wright. It was needless to try modes of breaking it to him. His fear made him leap at it as one under frenzy will leap down a precipice. I had no nerve for what I have no doubt followed, and hurried out just as he had thrown himself on his hard bed, and I heard his cries ringing behind the door as I again closed it.

Wright was brought to trial on a charge of wilful murder, with a minor charge of culpable homicide. It was a stretch to choose the latter; but the men were known to be friends, and as no one witnessed the catastrophe, the milder construction was put upon an act which, after all, I suspect was simply one of temporary madness. I doubt if all the strange particulars were ever known. Wright was sentenced to fourteen years' penal servitude. I have often thought of this case, but never diverged from the theory I mentioned to Wright himself. It does not affect my opinion of dreams. The two friends had been in the habit of getting into tilts, the result of their drinking. The dream was only an impression caused by some angry look forced out of the simple victim. The fever of the brain gave it consistency, and deepened it, and under the apprehension that he himself was to be stabbed, he stabbed his friend. This is the only dream-case in my book; and I'm not sorry for it, otherwise I might have glided into the supernatural, as others have done who have had more education than I, and are better able to separate the world of dreams from the stern world of realities.

The
Cock
and
Trumpet

❖

There are certain duties we perform of which we are scarcely aware, and which consist in a species of strolling supervision among houses, which, though not devoted to resetting, are often yet receptacles of stolen goods, through a mean of the residence there of women of the lowest stratum of vice and profligacy. Though we have no charge against the house at the time, and no suspicion that it contains stolen property, we claim the privilege of going through it on the ostensible pretence that we have in view a particular object of recovery. I have generally, I think, been fonder of these *pleasant* strolls than my brethren, perhaps for the reason that on some occasions I have been fortunate in what may be called chance waifs. Among these there was at the period I allude to, a well-known house, known as the Cock and Trumpet, for the reason that a bantam was represented on the sign as blowing the clarion of war in the shape of a huge French horn—significant no doubt of the crowing of the Gallic cockerel. It was a favourite of mine—the more by token that I had several times brought off rather wonderful things. On one occasion I issued triumphantly with a Dunlop cheese weighing thirty pounds, on another with a dozen of Italian sausages, and on another with two live geese.

It was a feature of the portly landlady that she never knew (not she) that such things were in the house. "Some of thae rattling deevils o' hizzies had done it. The glaikit limmers, will they no be content wi' their ain game, but maun turn common thieves?" Then her surprise was just as like the real astonishment as veritable wonder itself. "And got ye that in *my* house, Mr M'Levy? Whaur in a' the earth did it come frae? and wha brought it to the Cock and Trumpet? I wish I kent the gillet."

But the sound of *her* trumpet was changed one morning after she had taken to herself a certain Mr Alexander Dewar to be lord of her, her establishment, and the crowing bantam. Sandy, who was himself a great thief, had thus risen in the sliding scale. It is not often that thieves rise to be the head of an establishment with a dozen of beds, though without even a fir table by way of ordinary; but so true is the title of my book, that Sandy's slide upwards was just the cause of a return downwards with accelerated velocity.

One morning I happened to be earlier on my rounds than usual, and though houses like the Cock and Trumpet do their business during night, and are therefore late openers, I found the door open.

Something more than ordinary, I said to myself. The bantam must have been roused by some cock that has seen the morning's light sooner than it reaches the deep recesses of that wynd.

And going straight in, and passing through a room of sleeping beauties reposing blissfully amidst a chorus of snorts, I came to the bed-room of the new master himself. The mistress was enjoying in bed the repose due to her midnight and morning labours, snoring as deep as a woman of her size and suction could do, and beside her, in a chair, sat Sandy himself plucking lustily at fowls. He had finished nine hens, and was busy with the last of nine ducks. No wonder that the bantam had crown so early.

"What a fine show of poultry, Sandy, man," said I. "Where got you so many hens and ducks?"

"A man has surely a right to what comes into his ain trap," replied the rogue, as unmoved as one of the dead hens. "They flew in at the window."

And he proceeded with his operation of plucking.

My voice had in the meantime awakened his helpmate.

"Whaur can the hens hae come frae?" snorted the jolly woman. "Some o' the hizzies, nae doot."

"No, mistress," said I; "they flew in at the window."

"Weel, maybe they did."

"Just in the way the Bologna sausages did," said I.

"Na, it was the jade Bess Brown did that job, but I'm an innocent woman. Was I no sleeping when ye cam in? Does a sleeping woman catch hens in her sleep as she does flees in her mooth?"

"Well," said I, turning to Sandy, "you're the man."

"The Lord's will be dune," said the wife, in a tone quite at variance with her old system of asserting her innocence, (Sandy, her "husband", being bone of her bone and flesh of her flesh). "If Sandy has disgraced the house I made him master o', ay, and a gentleman to boot, he maun just dree the dregs."

Nor was I much surprised at this turn, for I had heard that she was losing conceit of Sandy, and had been repenting that she had raised him to the rank of a gentleman as well as lord of the Cock and Trumpet. Here was a good opportunity for getting quit of him, and the shrewd Jezebel saw her advantage.

"Now, Sandy," said I again to the cool rogue, still occupied with his work, and who had now arrived at the head feathers of the last duck, which head feathers (though generally left by poultry pluckers) I observed he had carefully taken from every victim: "lay down the duck and get a pillow-slip."

"Here's ane," cried his wife on the instant, as she began to undo the strings of her head cushion, ay, even that which had been frequently pressed by the head of her lord. "There," she added, as she threw the article out of the bed.

"Put these feathers into that bag," said I; "every feather, and I'll wait till I see the last put in."

"Ye'll find that a kittle job, Mr M'Levy. A fleeing feather's no easily catched."

"Weel," said Sandy, as he threw a wrathful glance at the mistress of his affection, now about to be lost to him, a loss of fifteen stones of solid beef—"I'll do your bidding," and then relaxing into a chuckle—"but will you tell me hoo the devil ony judge or jury can tell, after a' these feathers are mixed, which belongs to a duke, and which to a hen, and which to ae duke, and no to anither, and which to ae hen, and no to its neeghbour; and then after a' that, to whom the hens or the dukes belang? Ye see there's no a head feather left."

I saw in a moment that the cunning rogue had caught me, and that I might be in for an official scrape. But I had gone too far to recede, and I had got out of as great a difficulty before. "Put in the feathers quick," said I.

"The lasses will help him," cried the landlady, still bent on favouring the apprehension of Sandy; and quickly a husky voice sounded through the house, reaching, as it was intended, the hall of the sleeping beauties—"Kate Semple, Jessie Lumsdaine, Flora Macdonald."

And straightway came rushing from their beds two or three of her "children", as she used to call them. I need not describe the condition they were in, nor their swollen, sleepless eyes, their dishevelled hair, and their wondering looks, as they found their dreams probably changed from a place where there was roasting to a place of plucking.

"Help Sandy to put thae feathers in that pillow-slip, for the deil ane o' them will remain to tak' away the credit o' my house."

And thereupon the girls began the work, sprawling on their hands and knees, and putting in handful by handful as Sandy held open the mouth of the slip. The job was a difficult one, and the scene sufficiently picturesque to occupy my attention, diverted as it sometimes was by my anticipated difficulty in identifying the corpses; nor was it without a brush that they could accomplish the entire clearance I insisted on. Even the flying feathers I urged my nymphs to secure, an operation which they undertook with agility, screaming and laughing in the midst of their work with all that wild levity and recklessness for which their tribe is remarkable.

"Here," cried Mrs Dewar, "there's some on my bed." And commencing to pick them up, "Nae man shall say that a stown feather was left in my house."

A degree of refinement in this honest woman's purity which produced a smile from me, in spite of the difficulties of a case of evidence which promised me some trouble. Nor were my fears unreasonable. Our honour is at stake in such matters, and then we require to keep in view that while little good may result from punishing so determined and hardened a rogue as Sandy Dewar, the evil consequences of an acquittal are serious. It emboldens the culprit himself, and affords a triumph to the whole fraternity.

"And now, Sandy," said I, when there was scarcely a feather to be seen, "you'll bind all the legs of the corpses together."

A command which was obeyed slowly and reluctantly.

"Throw them over your back," continued I, "and the bag will go over all."

Having got my man laden with his dead spoil, "And now we'll march to the Office," said I.

"And fareweel, Sandy," cried a voice from the bed; "we'll maybe never see ane anither again. May the Lord prosper ye and mend ye!"

And finding matters in this favourable state, as I conceived, I bent my head over the lump of innocence:—

"Now, Mrs Dewar," whispered I, "just tell me how Sandy came by the ducks and hens."

"Aweel," said she in return, disappointing my hopes of an admission, "I'll say naething against my lawfu' husband. If the dukes and hens didna flee in at the window, it's now dead certain they'll no flee oot at the door."

These were the last words of the sonsy landlady, and I marched Sandy, with his burden, through an admiring crowd to the Office, where, having locked him up, I began to examine the dead bodies. The heads, as I have said, had been all taken care of, not a feather left upon one of them. Every corpse was so provokingly like another, that I could see no way of proving that they belonged to any one; and if, as was likely, Sandy had not been observed by any person about the place, I had no evidence to rest on but the equivocal words of Mrs Dewar, which pointed out no proprietor. I was in difficulty, but my difficulty was a stimulant as well; and there in the Office I sat, I know not how long, making my *post mortem* examination with all the assiduity of a doctor. My honour was concerned. The bantam would crow if my hens were not identified; but oh the inestimable virtue of perseverance! Were I to recount what this power has yielded me, I would read a lesson to the sluggard better than any imparted by Solomon. I had made my discoveries, and was the more satisfied with the result, as, during all the time I had been engaged in the examination of my eighteen dead bodies, I had become the theme of much good-humoured laughter among my compeers, joined in by the Superintendent and Lieutenant themselves.

A short time afterwards, there came in a charge from Mr Beaton, Hope Park, Meadows, to the effect that nine ducks had been stolen from his premises on the previous night; and after the lapse of another hour, a second charge, involving the nine hens, came from Mr Renton of Hope Park End. To these places I repaired, and saw the servants, who could, of course, have had no difficulty about the identity of their favourites, fed and tended by them every morning, and relieved by them of the succulent treasure they dropt so industriously for the morning's meal, provided the feathers remained, but they all laughed at the idea of knowing their lamented favourites with bare bodies. As to the thief, no one could say that he was seen, or even heard. Sandy had done his work well. I then got the lasses to dress themselves, and accompany me to the Office, where we soon arrived; the bodies were all lying in the state in which I left them. The sight to the girls was nothing less than striking. They held up their hands, and really looked pitiful, for no doubt they had had an affection for the creatures; and the strongest of us, I suspect, have some feelings thus lowly, but not the less sympathetically directed, which even the savoury morsel of a fed favourite cannot altogether dissipate. My pig is a better pig than yours; but I'd rather eat yours, if you will eat mine.

So the girls turned over and over the bodies, examining them with all the minuteness in their power. Jenny declared it impossible, and Helen was in despair; Peggy thought she observed something, and Barbara declared it to be nothing. I watched them with some amusement, nor less the men in the Office. They stood around us laughing heartily at the remarks of the investigators, running up a joke to a climax, and then pursuing another, not always at the sole expense of the lasses, who could retort cleverly, impeaching their mockers as utterly unable to distinguish a male from a female fowl. At the long run, a happy thought struck Jenny.

"But where's the 'pensioner?' " cried she.

"Ay, the 'pensioner,' " responded her neighbour Nelly.

"Had he a spliced leg?" inquired I.

"Yes," replied the first, "a dog broke it, and Nelly and I bound it up with two thin pieces of wood and a string."

"Ay, and he got aye the best handful of barley," rejoined Nelly; "but the leg of the 'pensioner' was cured a month ago, and the bandage removed."

"Is that the 'pensioner'?" said I, as I showed the leg of one which I had observed in the forenoon as having on it the appearance of a healed-up sore.

"Ay, just the creature," they both exclaimed. "It was the right leg, and you'll see yet the marks of the string."

The discovery was followed by the merriment of the men, who asserted that some one or other of the girls must have had a pensioner for a lover, with the designation of whom the drake had been honoured; but the girls indignantly denied the charge, declaring that they could not fancy a man pensioner, however much they might love a drake one.

"Besides," added Jenny, cleverly, "he was our pensioner, not the Queen's."

"So much for the ducks," said I; "and now for the hens and cocks; was there no pensioner among them?"

"No," cried Barbara, "but there was the 'corporal'."

"Any mark beyond the coat?" inquired I.

"Ay," cried Peggy, "he was stone-blind in the right eye; he lost his sight in a battle with Mr Grant's cock, and never recovered his eyesight again. When toying with his wives, he turned aye round to the left side."

"Yes," struck in Betty; "before his misfortune, he was the king of a' the cocks in the Meadows."

"Is that the blind 'corporal'?" said I.

"The very creature," cried Barbara, as she examined the white orb of the animal which I had detected in the morning; "but oh," she added, "I am vexed to see him in that condition!"

And really I thought I could see some little humidity about the blue eye of the good-natured girl.

"That's the lass for a man," thought I. "Give me a qualm of pity in a woman even for a bird, and I tell you you may make sure of a good wife."

I once knew—permit me to go off the scene a little—a young woman who lived in Great King Street. She was a great belle, and admired for a kind of beauty not uncommon among our servants. A gentleman in town, whose name I could mention, saw her one day, as she was carrying home some books from the library in Dundas Street. He was smitten—followed her—spoke to her—and entertained the idea of making her his wife, whereby she would have become a lady. Time passed; and, in the meantime, he was informed that the pretty Margaret one night, when in the bed-room flat of the house, pitched the cat, which had offended her in her cleanly notions, out of the window. It was a bitter cold night, and the frost was intense. In the morning the cat was found spiked on the railing, and frozen stiff. This was enough for our lover, and he forsook her. She afterwards fell, became a street-walker, and died neglected and uncared for in the Infirmary. I suspect the little pearl in Barbara's eye for the blind corporal was worth all the beauty in the face and person of the once admired but forsaken Margaret.

My story of the ducks and hens concludes with this investigation; for though the scene was renewed before the Sheriff, it was not so rich as that which took place among ourselves. Sandy got sixty days imprisonment for the ducks, and six months for the hens, as a kind of second offence; and Luckie Dewar could afford a few tears (common to certain amphibious animals on the banks of the Nile) over the misfortunes of Sandy Dewar, who had thus fallen from being master of the Cock and Trumpet to being the occupant of a prison. Such is the ascending and descending scale of profligate life.

The Widow's Last Shilling

❖

D o you know any one within the circle of your experience who is utterly renounced to himself—what is called a money-grub or hunks, eternally yearning for money, so as to deserve the address of Burns: "Fie upon you, coward man, that you should be the slave o't". If there's any tear about that man's eye, depend upon't it's only a thinnish rheum; and. as for anything like a response in the ear to the cry of pity, the drum will as soon crack at the singing of a psalm. Such a character is the result of an accumulation of *hardnesses,* increasing in intensity with his advancing years. We don't wonder so much at the hunks as hate him. But in regard to the brick-moulded thief, who seldom comes within the range of ordinary observation, you are apt to think that he is not so hard-hearted after all. You give him some credit for generosity,—nay, when he is picking your pocket, you lay to his charge more necessity than will. Yet there never was a harder-hearted wretch than a regular thief. He is as destitute of pity as of honesty, and will steal as readily the shilling from under the poorhouse pensioner's pillow as the ring from the finger of my lady. Even after "feeding time" he is still rapacious, and if he ever gives away, it is from recklessness, never from benevolence.

I have had many cases that go to prove these remarks, and one occurs to me worthy of recital, from the personal proximity into which I was brought to the condition of the hearts of the actors.

In the eddies at the bottoms of stairs leading to pawnshops, a detective has often a chance for promising rises to his phantom

minnow. In 1845, somewhere in August, I chanced to be coming up
the stair leading from the Market to Milne Square. Just as I was
arriving at the passage out, two women were coming down from the
Equitable Loan Company's Office; and as they were engaged in
conversation, I stood a few steps down where I couldn't be seen,
and heard what they were saying to each other. The voices were
those of a young brisk wench and an aged woman, with that kind of
wail in her speech which sometimes comes to be a bad habit, but
which at least shows that the heart is not so easy as it might be.

"I got five shillings on a plaid worth five pounds," said the
younger. "What did he give you on the blankets?"

"No less than I sought," replied the elder, "ten shillings. It will
just pay my landlord, and leave a shilling over; but it's a sore heart
to me to pawn, for I never was used to it; yet better pawn than be
poinded."

"And who will poind you ?"

"My landlord for the rent, woman; ay, a rich man with thousands, who feeds his servants on roast-beef and pudding till they
are ready to burst, and yet takes the two or three shillings of rent of
me which I need for porridge; and it's not that these great people
like their servants, only they like to get the name of their house
being a good meat-house; and the fat limmers are as saucy to them,
after all, as ever."

"But where have you put your ten shillings?" said the other.
"Take care you don't lose it. Is it in your pocket?"

"Ay, all safe enough, along with the ticket. If I lose them, I lose
all; and I may just as weel be coffined at once, and be done wi't.
Ye're a young creature, and don't know the miseries o' the old."

"And don't want for a while," said the other; "but where do you
live?"

"In Lady Lawson's Wynd," was the reply.

"And how do you go home?"

"By Hunter Square and the Bridge," said the simple woman;
"for I've to go to Nicolson Square, where the factor lives, to pay
him the nine shillings; but I doubt if he will ever get more, for now,

with my blankets in the pawn, and nothing to redeem them, what is to cover me in the cold nights of winter?"

"What you can get, woman," said the other, harshly, as I thought, at least without the feeling due to age and poverty; "just as I do, what we all do—the world to the winner."

And what heartless creature can this young woman be? thought I, as, making a long neck, I looked round the side of the stair. My five-times convicted Mary Anne Stewart, one of the nimblest pick-pockets of the city, and for whom I was then looking as connected with a stolen plaid.

"Easy to say that," continued the old woman, "when you've health and youth on your side; but don't be too confident. I was once a winner when I won my poor husband; but what was there for me to win when I lost him who was the winner of my bread, and was left to fight the battle of life with nothing but my ten fingers? You've both to win and to lose yet, my lass; and may the Lord be kinder to you than He has been to me!"

"Best to look to one's-self and one's own pocket," was the consistent reply of the winner, Mary Anne.

And to the pockets of others, said I to myself, the graceless baggage.

"And you never look to Heaven, lass?" again said the woman.

"Never got anything from that quarter yet," was the reply, in the same strain. "Will Heaven enable you to take that pawn-ticket out of your pouch and get your blankets back?"

"Ay, and maybe mair," said the woman; "but though Providence may look sour on me, there's the Lord of providence, lass, mind that; and He can smile on you even when you're suffering, for He knows He can take you out of it. And what church go ye to with these notions in your head?"

"No one," was the saucy answer; "there's no kail in the kirks ;" then with a laugh, "The ministers eat all the showbread."

And what more of this kind of talk which I have reported, perhaps in a form different from what took place, but retaining the general sentiments of both, I cannot say, for they moved off. I saw them still at it in the midst of the square, and till they came to the end of the close opposite Hunter Square, where they parted. Meanwhile I went down the steps by the Bridge, and making a circle round, I saw the woman making for Hunter Square, where there was a crowd round an Italian with a puggy—general holding a levee—a more sensible animal than its master. Then keeping my eye on Mary Anne, I saw her join William Walker and James M'Guire, two of my very best friends, as ready to do me a service now as they had done before on more occasions than one. They did not seem at the moment to be in so playful a mood as the Italian's puggy; and I did not look for much sport till I got my expectations sharpened by their movement after Mrs Kerr (that was the name, I think) towards the two mountebanks, who had removed to the south of the Tron.

I then wheeled round the north-east corner of the church, and keeping my eye on my trio, I placed myself in a stair-foot on the east side of the South Bridge, from which I could see both sets of performers, as well as those performed upon. Mrs Kerr, who, in Lady Lawson's Wynd, had no opportunity of seeing monkeys from her garret window, seemed to have forgotten the sorrows of her rent-day and the pawn-shop, and was gaping, as all sight-seers do, at the evolutions of pug, one of whose best feats, general as he was, was to extract his master's pocket handkerchief from the one pocket of his cotton velvet coat and put it in the other, and then came the laugh, in which, I presume, the widow of the sorrowful face joined, when the Italian sought for the article in the wrong pocket. Mrs Kerr did not take the lesson, though the Italian, as a kind of philanthropist, might have had the credit of putting his crowd upon their guard. The simple woman, from whose mind all her sorrows seemed, for the moment, banished, enjoyed this trick wonderfully, for I could see the careworn face lighted up with the very extreme of satisfaction. Mary Anne was now at her back, apparently gaping too, and behind her stood Walker and M'Guire, as interested in pug's pocket-picking as if the trick had been one new to them, and worthy of being learned.

Now I fairly admit that, while I expected something, I was utterly unprepared for an attack on Mary Anne's part on her poor old friend of the entry; for however harsh her words were to the old woman, I still thought she had some qualms of pity excited in her by that sorrowful wail which had struck my own ears as something touching and heart-stirring. I had been simply false to my experience, while Mary Anne remained true to her heartless craft. Yes, I saw the young hopeless extract from Mrs Kerr's pocket something, doubtless the ten shillings, and hand it to M'Guire, whereupon they all three hurried away down the High Street.

My energy was roused in a moment, sharpened by the cruelty of this most heartless robbery. My course was, to myself, clear, though not, perhaps, what you might imagine. I have always had a horror of being seen rushing along the street, like Justice under hysterics flying after a victim. It's not decorous, and, besides, it does no good. The red-hand is a good catch, but I have often enough known a startled thief drop a valuable which never could be recovered, and I have found my account better balanced by knowing my man, and catching him with the booty, when he thinks all safe. In this case, I allowed the three to pass me, nor did I lay hands on them. I first hurried up to Mrs Kerr, and touching her on the shoulder,

"Is your ten shillings safe in your pocket?" said I.

"My ten shillings!" said she, nervously; "surely it is, but how do you know I had ten shillings in my pocket?"

"Never mind that, search quick."

"The Lord help me!" she exclaimed, as she fumbled in her empty pocket; "it's gone, with the pawn-ticket. I'm ruined, sir; it's all I have in the world, and how am I to meet the factor? I'm ruined, ruined!"

And she burst into tears, sobbing in the midst of the crowd.

"Get as fast as you can to the Police-Office," said I, "and I'll bring to you the pickpockets, and maybe your money. You know one of them."

"Who could be so cruel?" she inquired.

The young woman you blabbed to in the pawnbroker's stair," said I.

"Oh, the Lord forgive her," said she, "for I told her the whole story of my grief."

"Which you should have kept to yourself," said I. "Away to the Office, and wait for me."

And having seen her off I proceeded down the High Street, in the direction taken by the thieves. That confidence I have so often felt, and perhaps somewhat vaingloriously expressed, I can account for in no other way than viewing it as a result of my knowledge of thieves and their haunts, joined to the impression of so many successes. On this occasion I was so sure, that I believed I walked as if I had been going to dinner, without being quickened by a very sharp appetite; but I did not feel the less desire to get hold of those who had so unknowingly to themselves roused sympathies in my breast, made sluggish, no doubt, by the hardening influences of official routine. Mary Anne was so well known about the High Street, that she couldn't pass without the observation of the loungers in that crowded resort of the poor. A few passing hints, like dots in a line, led me along till I came to Toddrick's Wynd, at the head of which I paused, and casting a glance down with my advantage of a good eye for a long wynd, I saw one of those little clots of human beings, generally so interesting to me, in proportion as they show an interest among themselves. I was quicker now, and rushing forward, I came upon the three I wanted, all busy in the glorious ceremony of division, that is, giving every one *his own*, with the exception of the proprietor. The very sums were in their hands, with the unction inseparable from the acquisition of money.

"Five shillings to Mary Anne, and half-a-crown to each of you," said I, "is fair. I will settle it for you, since you seem to disagree. The pawn-ticket for the blankets is for my trouble."

There is seldom any hurry-skurry among these gentry, for they know the worst, and are made up to it.

"Come, give me the money."

And so they did, the whole ten shillings, and the ticket to boot.

"No kail in the police cell to night, Mary Anne," said I, "any more than in the church, where the ministers eat all the showbread."

Mary Anne looked into my face, and burst out into a laugh,— such is the seared and hardened temperament of thieves; and it is as well that the punishment-mongers should know this, that they may endeavour to devise some other and more effectual mode of reclamation.

"So you had no pity for the poor old woman?"

"The whining hag had more money than I had," was the reply.

"You mean more than the five shillings you got for the stolen plaid?" said I.

"Who said it was stolen?"

"The lady in Gilmour Place you stole it from," said I. "I have been looking for you to settle that small matter for three days."

A streak of new light thus thrown upon an old subject, which qualified Mary Anne's fun, and silenced her.

At this moment my assistant came up, and we took the three to the Office, where I brought the young thief to face with Mrs Kerr. The look of relief which played over the grief-worn features of the woman when she saw her four half-crowns and pawn-ticket, can only be understood by those who are, or have been, poor, and who know the narrow margin on the verge of which flit the few and des- ultory illumined figures of their happiness. It did not last long, for it was to give place to the old melancholy, but I believe the feelings with which she looked on the face of the hardened creature to whom she had poured out the simple history of her sorrows, would never pass away.

"I didn't think, for all I have heard of the wickedness of human creatures," she said, as she kept her eyes on Mary Anne, who did not seem to feel her situation more than as quite a natural one, "that it was in the heart of a woman to rob one, who might be her mother, of all she had in the world."

"'Twill learn you to look at monkeys again," replied Mary Anne, with a laugh, which gave so ludicrous a turn to the pathetic, that the Lieutenant himself could scarcely resist it.

She might have profited by the monkey, thought I, for it offered her a lesson which she did not take to heart.

And thus this act of the strange drama ended. The next was the retributive one—the issue or conclusion being proportioned, not to the amount taken, but to the enormity of the hardened depravity which it revealed. The three were tried before the High Court. Mary Anne, as the principal performer, getting ten years' transportation, and Walker and M'Guire seven years each. So that, has Mary Anne's mind not been closed against every good impression, she would have admitted that, if she had never previously obtained anything from that Power she so irreverently maligned, she had at length received a share of the stern and severe reward it invariably bestows upon the vicious and the guilty.

The
Happy
Land

D on't fancy I am going to speak of the "happy land" of which Richard Weaver sings so well, through the medium of the hymn, so joyous with its "away and away" to where many of us, it is to be hoped, have mothers, and sisters, and brothers. Nor will the people of Edinburgh be ignorant of the meaning of the title of my present reminiscence. Yet many may not know the "happy land" I allude to—not other than that large tenement in Leith Wynd, not far from the top, composed of a number of houses, led to by a long stone-stair,—the steps of which are worn into inequalities by the myriads of feet, tiny and large, light and heavy, steady and unsteady, which have passed up and down so long,—and divided into numerous dens, inhabited by thieves, robbers, thimblers, pick-pockets, abandoned women, drunken destitutes, and here and there chance-begotten brats, squalling with hunger, or lying dead for days after they should have been buried. Well do I know every hole and corner of it, and so well that I shrink from a description of it, which at the best would be only a mass of blotches—not a picture, only coarse cloth and dingy paint. Some people may have a notion of a "stew"; but the Happy Land is a great conglomeration of stews; so that the scenes, the doings, the swearings, the fights, the drunken brawls, the prostitutions, the blasphemies, the cruelties, and the robberies, which you figure of various houses removed by distance, are often all going on at the same moment, and with no more screens or barriers to hide the shame than thin lath walls and crazy doors—often, indeed, without any division at all. Yet all the people who inhabit this accumulation of dens understand each other. It is a world by itself, with no law ruling except force, no compunction

89

except fear, no religion except that of the devil. They laugh at every thing that is fair and good, and transfer the natural feelings due to these over to evil; and, then, there's not a whit of effort in all this— to them it is perfectly natural. And I'm not sure if they do not consider the outside world over in the New Town a very tame affair, not worth living for.

In the third storey of the huge tenement, as you go into the right, there was a section of this little world, occupied by a young, stout, and fair hizzy, called Mary Wood, about twenty years of age. She was well known, not only in the Happy Land itself, but in Princes Street, where she was often seen walking as demurely under her fashionable bonnet as any of the young ladies from the houses in the New Town. Her section was very limited, consisting only of a small room, containing a bed, a table, a chair or two, a looking-glass of course, and a trunk for her fineries, not forgetting "the red saucer". Immediately off this room was a closet, with no means of light, excepting one or two auger-bored holes, intended for gratifying any one taking up his station there by a look of what was going on in the room. These two apartments formed the castle of this enchantress, and the scene of a plot—not uncommon then—entered into by Mary and two strong ruffians of the names of George Renny and James Stevenson. The conspiracy was not so complicated as it was bold, dastardly, and cruel. Mary was to go out in her most seductive dress, and endeavour to entice in any gentleman likely to have a gold watch and money on him, and when she had succeeded in this, the two bullies, as they have been called, who, on a signal of her approach, had previously betaken themselves to the closet, were, when they considered all matters ripe, to rush out, seize the victim, and rob him.

This conspiracy, I had reason to suspect, had been carried on for some time with considerable success, and without our being applied to by the sufferers, many of whom were anxious to conceal their imprudence, and consented rather to lose their watches than expose their character. One night, the 9th of August 1849, our damsel was trying her fortune in Princes Street, while Renny and Stevenson were waiting, ready for their work when the time came. About twelve o'clock, she fascinated a likely "cully", or "colley", as the Scotch women say, with perhaps more humour than they wot of—a gentleman of the name of W———n, from London, who, little knowing the character of the "happy land" to which he was destined, agreed to accompany her home. In a short time she had him all safe. Mistress of her trade, she was all blandishments to the happy Englishman, who, after all deductions for the squalor of her dwelling, could probably not have picked up a woman better qualified to please; but no sooner had he made preparations for departing, than the gentlemen of the dark closet rushed out upon him, laid him on his back, took from him a gold watch and chain, with fifteen sovereigns, and everything they could rifle; but, most unkind cut of all, the enchantress Mary helped them in their work of robbery, pulling off his fingers two valuable rings, which, a little before, she was praising to him with much admiration. I afterwards ascertained that the struggle was a desperate one, no doubt owing to the value of the property inflaming the one party, and nerving the other.

When allowed to depart, Mr W———n, much injured, and greatly alarmed, rushed down-stairs, almost breaking his neck in the descent, and went direct to the Police-office, where he gave a rapid account of the transaction, as well as a description of the parties. The case was one for me, and, about one o'clock, I was roused out of my sleep to catch these robbers. I recollect I was much wearied that day, and was in no humour for a midnight hunt, exhausted, as I had been, by late hours. I was, not withstanding, dressed in a moment. I went first to see the gentleman, who seemed inclined to lose more time by a description. I told him it was of no use, for that I knew the men perfectly. I had, indeed, seen them in company with Mary, who was familiar to me, and knew that they were her special retainers. The difficulty was to know where to find them, and get hold of the money, but I had confidence enough to tell Mr W———n that, if he would remain for a time in the office, I would bring the robbers to him. As for Mary, she had been taken up about the time I was called, but she had no money on her—the whole having been carried off by the robbers.

My task was arduous enough, for, although I knew their haunts, the places were not few, and would likely be avoided. I tried many without success, and was beginning to repent of my promise to Mr W———n, when I bethought me of a lodging-house at the West Port, occupied by a man of the name of Goodall. Thither I went. It was now about four in the morning, and having rapped, I was answered from behind the door by Goodall.

"Did two men come to your house this morning to lodge?" was my question.

"Yes," replied he, as he opened the door, probably knowing my voice.

"Well, I think they will be the men I want."

"But you're too soon," said Goodall, with a kind of laugh.

"Why?"

"Because it's only *four*, and they told me they were not to be wakened till five."

"That's a pity," said I; "but they will excuse *you*, and as for me, why they set me up at one, so I'm quits with them there. Show me into their room."

I then beckoned the constable I had with me; and, preceded by Goodall, we were led to the side of the bed where lay the very men. I held Goodall's candle over their faces, and saw the effect I produced upon them—not that I augured from their surprise and dismay that they had done this deed, for I knew I was a terror to them at any time, but that I liked to enjoy my advantage.

"Get up," said I, "and go with me;" so sure of my men, that I did not even put them to the question.

And then broke in Goodall again with his humour—

"Ye see, ye're not to blame me, my lads. It's only four, but Mr M'Levy says you were the cause of wakening him at one."

These men, who, four hours before, were throttling an innocent gentleman, were now dumb and docile; nay, they were simple,— for Renny, when getting out of bed, let slip—

"You'll not find either the watch or the sovereigns on me, any-how."

Stevenson looked daggers at his friend.

"Why, man," said I, "Renny has done no more than I have made others do, by simply holding my peace; and he has done you no harm either by his mistake, for I can prove that you and Mary Wood robbed the gentleman four hours ago in the Happy Land."

"D——n the Happy Land," cried Stevenson, still enraged at his friend. "I never found any happiness in it, nor money either."

"D——n the Happy Land!" said Goodall, again wishing to be witty. "Lord save us! that's a terrible oath against a place we are all doing our best to get to. The very children sing, 'Come to you happy land,' and you curse it."

I could scarcely keep from laughing, even in the midst of my impatience, at the keeper of this famous resort for all moral waifs thus reproving, by his mirth, his children,—so many of whom came from that Happy Land. Of course he had reason to bless it, and did it in his own way of humour—a habit of his.

"Quick," said I, as the putting on of the clothes proceeded slowly. "Mr W——n is waiting for you."

Worst shock yet, for such men are great moral cowards; and to confront the gentleman they treated so cruelly was so complete a turn, within so short a time, that my words stunned them.

In a quarter of an hour after they were standing before Mr W——n.

"Are these your men?" said I.

"Ah, I know them too well," said the gentleman. "And I wish I had never seen them; for I am a stranger here,—all my money is gone, and I know not what to do."

"We have none of your money," replied Stevenson growlingly.

No doubt secreted somewhere. I forgot to say I searched them at Goodall's.

"And it is gone, then?" said Mr W——n, despondingly.

"No," said I; "not all. The money may not be recovered easily, but I will get the watch."

"Well, I shall live in hope," said Mr W——n, as he went away, leaving his address.

They were now locked up, and the next question for me was how to get the property.

On the following and subsequent days every effort was made. There had been no pledging or selling to the brokers, and I was at fault; but I had succeeded in so many cases where there appeared no hope, that I persevered. As a last resource, I had a young fellow confined for a short time along with the prisoners, who I knew was on terms of intimacy with them. All thieves and robbers "split" when in trouble; confidences are the weakness of criminal natures; yet, perhaps, I would not have got this information if he had not expected I would favour him. He told me that the two men, after having committed the robbery, flew along St Mary's Wynd and never stopped till they got to the Dumbiedykes;—that there they placed the watch, sovereigns, and rings into a hole of the old dyke, where they made a secret mark, only known to themselves.

I was now as much at fault as ever. The men remained obdurate, and they alone knew the secret. I would, however, try the old dyke; and while I was busy peering into the crevices, who should come up to me but one of the park-keepers?

"I think," said he, "I know what you are looking for. You're Mr M'Levy?"

"Yes," said I. "I am searching for a stolen watch and sovereigns; can you help me to the place?"

"I can, at least, help you to the watch," said he, as he held out the glittering object, with its gold chain and seals. "I found it here," he continued, going a few steps along. "The rainy night must have washed away the earth from the top of the dyke, for I found it nearly exposed in a hole not deep enough to escape observation."

And so the watch was recovered, but no more. The sovereigns were never found, and are likely in that dyke to this day, for all the three prisoners were shortly after transported for seven years.

The
Wrong
Shop

❖

It is only a state of *civilisation* that can produce so strange a relation as that between detectives and robbers. In any other condition of society it is inconceivable, for love is almost always mutual, and hatred reciprocal in rude states; and it is not very easy to conceive a condition where one party follows and seeks from a spirit of well-wishing, and another curses and flies from a spirit of hatred. If there is any one we wish to see more than another, it is a robber; and if there is any creature out of the place of four letters a robber wishes to be away from, it is an officer of the law. It may seem strange enough if I should be able to give a case where this was reversed, in a manner which has sometimes forced from me a laugh.

In 1847, a house in Minto Street, and another in Claremont Crescent, were broken into, and robbed of a vast number of portable articles of great value. The families had left the houses to go to the country; and the robbers, being aware that there was nobody to disturb them, had gone about their selection of articles with much artistic deliberation and skill, taking only those things which could be melted, such as silver utensils, or altered or dyed, such as silk dresses, shawls, and the like. We got intimation first of the Minto Street affair, for it was some time before it came to be known even to the proprietor that the house in Claremont Street had been disturbed. Having got my commission, I very soon came to the conclusion that, for a time at least, there could be no discovery by tracing the articles; and just as soon to another, that the whole were secreted, probably in a mass, in some of the lodging-houses resorted to by the gang—for that there was a gang I had no manner of doubt—

nor was I at a loss about some of the component parts of the crew,—
at least I knew that one or two well-known housebreakers had been
seen in the city, and their affinities are almost a matter of course
with us.

There was ingenuity, therefore, required in this affair beyond
the mere care in dogging some of the artists to their dormitories,
and this I soon accomplished by tracing Jane Walker, one of their
callets, to the house of one Sim at the West Port. Other bits of intelligence contributed to the conclusion, that Sim's house was the
sleeping place of some of them, and the rendezvous of the whole
pack. As I have already said, I have always had a craving for a full
haul when I put out my net, and take my seat in the cobble to see
the wily tribe get into the meshes. So on this occasion I made my
arrangements with this view.

At a late hour one night I took with me several constables and
proceeded to Sim's house. I arranged my men in such a way that
egress was scarcely possible, while some one would be ready to
help me inside in the event of an emergency; for it is no indifferent
affair to go bang in upon an entire gang of desperate burglars, especially when there are women among them—a remark which requires merely this explanation, that the women egg up the men to
resistance, and the men have often a desire to show off their prow-
ess before their dulcineas.

Having presented myself at Sim's door, I heard a shout of merriment, indicative of a goodly company; and I confess the sound,
though rough and brutal, was rather pleasant to me, for it satisfied
me they were all there, and, moreover, off their guard, through the
seduction of their tender dalliances. I am often fine in my self-
introductions, but here I found my cue in bluntness. I opened the
door with a sudden click of the sneck, and stood before as motley a
crew of ruffians and viragoes as I ever remember to have seen. Nor
was the effect all on one side. If I was amazed at seeing such a
collection of celebrities, they were not less astonished at seeing
me. Laughter did not need to hold her sides, nor Mockery to twist
her chaps into mows, nor even Inebriety to flare up into a rage. All

was quiet in an instant, with every eye fixed upon me as Sim himself, James M'Culloch, John Anderson, Hector M'Sally, James Stewart, Agnes Hunter, Sarah Jack, Christian Anderson, and Jane Walker, had been all too well accustomed to such blandishments as mine, to be thrown off their guard beyond the instant of the working of the first charm. They simply took me for a devil, who might seize their bodies for punishment, but could not insist upon their pledges to be his for ever. In short, they knew the extent of my power, as well as their necessities to resist it, but only if resistance could be successful.

I had stopt their merriment;—but just allow me, as I stand for a moment before them, to say, it is no merriment that these strange beings enjoy: their hearts have no part in their laughter, which is a mere dry shaking of the lungs, and better named as a cackle, or sometimes a vociferation. It is almost always the result of a personal gibe; for there is no real friendship to restrain them, and their art is a deadly fly that kills at the first leap. They seem to find some relief from the tearing devil within, by tearing their brother devils without; and though it is done under the semblance of fun, it is as cruel and wicked as they can make it, But then the very cruelty in the personality gets applause; the laugh rings, and every one has his turn to be quizzed and gibed—the bearing of which, again, is a kind of stern virtue among them. It is all a heart-burning, with a flickering ebullition over the surface; and the effort seems to be to produce Pain, and yet to make it pass as a kind of pleasure. I know them well; and could, at a distance, distinguish between the merriment of people with sound hearts, and that of these artificial beings, as well as I could do were I among them, and knew the two sets of characters.

A moment sufficed for my introduction.

"There are some things that have gone amissing," said I, "and I want to know whether any of them are here."

"Nothing," said Sim; but the manner of his "nothing" showed me it was a misnomer for "something."

"No harm in seeing. I don't charge any of you, but I may just say that you are as safe in your seats there, as you could be if you had wings and used them. I have friends at the door, so—quiet. Sim, I want to speak with you in the other room. Get a candle."

All authority lies in bearing. The man obeyed like a machine, got his dip lighted, and followed me into the small room, (there were only two in the house,) when I took the light from him, with the intention of looking into hidden places, but there was strangely enough no necessity for searching. There before me stood a huge trunk or box, more like a coal bunker or ship's locker than a chest, and sufficient to have held within its capacious sides a jeweller's stock. Knocking my foot against it, and finding it heavy with contents,

"Why," said I, "how comes this to be here?"

"All right," replied the man; "nothing of yours there."

"Let me see," said I. "Get me the key."

"The key is with the proprietor," said he, coolly. "Why you know, sir, it's an emigrant's box that there, and he has merely left it with me till the ship sails, when he will return for it—all right."

"And there's nothing in it belonging to these gentry in the kitchen?"

"Not a handkerchief."

"Well," said I, "as I don't wish this trunk to *emigrate* before I know what's inside, I will break it open."

And going into the kitchen, I seized a big salamander, standing by the fire, and without saying a word to the no doubt wondering company, who were working hard to look easy, I returned to the room. Up to this kind of work, I managed, by getting a lever point for my poker, to send the top of the box in splinters in a very few minutes, but with a crash which, like the laughter of my friends in the kitchen, had more sound than music in it. And lo! there was a sight—a veritable curiosity box—a bazaar in miniature; in short, as I afterwards ascertained, all the valuables abstracted not only from the house in Minto Street, but from that in Claremont Crescent, had been brought together, as if by the hand of Prospero's little friend, for my gratification, and yet with no bidding from me.

I had taken a large liberty, and I must take a larger to justify the first. I had provided myself with some of Mrs M'G—r's marks—the lady in Minto Street—so I straightway began to turn out the fine poplins and silks, which overlaid the jewellery at the bottom, till I could find a handkerchief or some article bearing a name, and that I very soon did, in a damask towel, bearing "M'G. 6."

I was now relieved from all fears of a misused freedom.

"All right," said I.

And going to the door, I called on my men. There was here a little mismanagement. They were not so close as they should have been, and M'Sally and Stewart, the real burglars, getting desperate, jostled the first officer, and pushing him up against the wall, escaped; nor were the other men sufficiently on the alert to be able to intercept them, so that they got themselves reserved, as it were, for a fate which is the real burden of my story.

The trunk, and all the remaining members of the gang, were straightway under better keeping than that of Mr Sim, who considered all *so* right; but I had to lament the want of my *chiefs*, the very men on whom my mind was set, and for whom I would have given the whole contents of the locker; but I was not to be done out of them by a mere flight, which did not exclude me from a long shot, and that shot I proceeded to prepare. The prior history of M'Sally enabled me to suspect that he was away down by the east coast to get to London, and I had no doubt Stewart would accompany him, so I straightway got the Lieutenant to forward their portraits to Berwick-on-Tweed, Newcastle, and Shields, with directions to the different Lieutenants to seize and send them back, to Edinburgh, where they were specially wanted. As matters turned out, this was a happy suggestion, and proved a comfort to me after my distress.

My gentlemen, just as I suspected, had made their way down to Berwick, with very little money as it appeared, yet with such a locker at home, upon which they had expected to live and feast for many months, (alas, the vanity of human wishes!) and arrived there pretty late at night. They, of course, wanted lodgings, and why should they not get them for nothing, where the philanthropic people of the old town, reversing their former fire-eating character, had prepared the town-hall, of ancient renown for bellicose orations, as a place of refuge for the destitute. The two refugees were even in their misfortunes inclined to be humorous, and took it into their heads to act the part of industrious "tramps," travelling to the south in search of work, and apply for a night's lodging at the very town-hall itself. But who had the privilege of giving out the tickets? Why, who better qualified than the Superintendent of Police himself, who could, from his office, make the proper distinction between the really deserving applicants, and those to whom a jail was a more fitting place of abode? And so it was the Superintendent had the charge of the house of refuge as well as the house of bondage. They had run away for housebreaking, and escaped the fiend M'Levy, and there was a neat squareness in playing off a trick upon his brother of Berwick. A glimpse of the sunshine of fun comes well after the gloom of misfortune; besides, sweet is refuge to the houseless; and then a supper and a breakfast was not to be despised.

They were accordingly soon brought before the dispenser of refuge and justice, who was busy at the time scanning a paper.

"Poor workmen, sir, going south in search of work," said M'Sally; "would your honour pass us to the town hall?"

"Where from?" said the Superintendent.

"Aberdeen."

"Your names?"

"James M'Intosh and John Burnet," was the reply.

"Blue coat and grey trousers," muttered the Superintendent, as he looked at the paper—"blue coat and grey trousers," he repeated, as he glanced at M'Sally. "Monkey jacket and buff vest," looking again at the paper—"monkey jacket and buff vest," directing his eyes to Stewart.

"We have been travelling all day, sir," said Stewart, and are weary; please pass us on."

But the Superintendent was in no hurry.

"Grey eyes and foxey whiskers," he muttered, again getting more curious, as he read and looked, and looked and read, still going over features—"sharp nose, grey eyes, fiery-coloured whiskers—dark eyes and black whiskers"—and so forth, until at last he came to the conclusion—"the very men."

"Yes," he said, as he rose and touched a small bell, "I will pass you, but not to the town-hall of Berwiek."

"Any other quarters for poor destitutes will do, sir," said Stewart.

"What think you of the police-office of Edinburgh," said the Superintendent, "where you, Hector M'Sally and Joseph Stewart, are, according to this paper I have in my hands, and which I got just as you entered, charged with breaking into a house in Minto Street, and another in Claremont Crescent, and stealing therefrom many valuable articles."

"We are not the men," said the two, determinedly.

"Read your paper again; sir," said M'Sally, "and compare, and you'll find we are not the men."

The Superintendent was taken aback, and did look again.

"Would you read out the description?" said M'Sally.

"I think you have got on a blue coat and grey trousers," said the Superintendent.

"Yes, sir."

"And you have got grey eyes and foxey whiskers?"

"No, sir; black eyes and black whiskers."

"And you," said the Superintendent, a little put out, turning to Stewart, "you have a monkey-jacket and buff vest?"

"Yes, sir."

"And black eyes and beard?"

"No, sir; grey eyes and light whiskers."

"Well, then, how stand your noses? You"—to M'Sally—"have a turned-up one, and a little awry, I think?"

"And you"—to Stewart—"have a very long one, raised in the middle?"

"Yes, sir.

"Well, well; suppose the clothes of the one put upon the other—it was easy for you to change them—and we have you to a button.

Bertram, pass these gentlemen to a cell for the night, and I shall get them sent off to Edinburgh in the morning."

Next day we had a letter setting forth the dodge of the exchange, and the curious way they had fallen into the hands of the Superintendent. It was thence an easy business to get our two gentlemen to go to the right shop—Norfolk Island—after having tried the wrong one at Berwick. They and Anderson were transported for seven years. M'Culloch was acquitted.

The
Letter

❖

It would be a lucky thing for thieves and robbers, when they are suspected, that people should make no inquiries after them; but, just as if they became of greater importance by guilt, their friends seem often inclined to feel greater interest in them—a tendency which has often resulted very favourably to me. In June 1847, Josiah Milstead, a clerk in a pawn-office at Woolwich, absconded with a sum of £60, a quantity of valuable jewellery, and many articles of wearing apparel. Information was sent to various towns, among the rest to Edinburgh. We had of course the ordinary description of the person of Milstead, to which I gave my best study; but there was not such a peculiarity in his face and appearance as to form a good representation in my mind, so as that I could seize him, if I met him promiscuously. I required in a case of this kind to be wary, lest I should pounce upon some gentleman, and bring trouble upon myself, as well as injure the *prestige* of the force for prudence and perspicuity.

I have seldom found that a runaway does not leave some trace of where he is to be found with some person, who is dear to him either through relationship or love; or, if his flight has been sudden, he will find some means of telling that person where he is. It is from such considerations that we are so often led to the vestibule of the Post-office, where we smell for other odours than that of the musk which so often perfumes that place, as a kind of memory left by love-letters to those who send them away so hopefully. I was accordingly on my post there, and soon observed a young man of genteel appearance and placid, if not melancholy countenance, who seemed to me to come dangerously within the description of my man. He called at the counter, and, finding no letter, came out to the vestibule; and, as a matter of course—though at present it would,

I was aware, do me no good, for he would get no letter addressed to
him in his own name—I ascertained from the clerk, that he had
asked for a letter to a certain address, which I now forget. I instantly again got to the vestibule, where I found him hanging about
with a melancholy look upon his face, suggesting to me that he was
a waif, and did not know what to make of himself; but I had other
motives for loving him, for every time I looked at him, I was the
more certain he was the object on whom my heart ought to have
been fixed, and was fixed. Yet I did not feel myself authorised to
embrace him; not that I was a bashful lover, but a prudent one, who
would make sure against a rejection, with perhaps an insult.

While thus keeping my eye on him with the view of seeing him
home,—an attention I have bestowed on many who never thanked
me for it,—I observed among the crowd one or two pickpockets;
and, what was more strange, these light-fingered gentry seemed to
be as fond of my swain as I was myself—a circumstance altogether
singular, as in general they have very good reasons for bestowing
their favours on those to whom I show the greatest indifference.
Watching them with even more interest than I generally feel, I saw
one of them jerk a pocket-handkerchief out of one of his outer pockets, and at the same instant a letter fell out upon the ground. I
instantly seized the pickpocket; but just as instantly, my interesting gentleman of the melancholy face picked up the letter, and
making a bolt, was off. The whole affair occupied only an instant. I
found that I had committed a slight mistake. If I had cared less
about the pickpocket than the letter, I would likely have had my
man; but at least I had got something—the handkerchief; and, what
was more, I got my suspicions of my man confirmed to a certainty,
because, if that letter had not been sufficient to betray him, he
never would have made off, and left the silk handkerchief behind
him.

Having taken the pickpocket to the office, I began to think of
the singularity of this occurrence—what if this handkerchief, so
wonderfully thrown before me as it were, should turn out to be a
part of the stolen property? That could soon be ascertained, but

then in the meantime I might lose my man. I must, therefore, try to fall in with him again, trusting to the rule that lovers meet, by some kind of chance, oftener than other people; but just while intending to take one of my contemplative walks, I learned at the office a piece of information which altered my scheme. A letter had come from Woolwich, stating that Milstead had a sweetheart there, who had been indiscreet enough to let out that she corresponded with him under a name which he had found means to convey to her. That name was enclosed, and what was my astonishment to find that it was the very one given me by the clerk at the Post-office? And here, too, was the rare example of two lovers after the same man, and yet one of them not only not jealous, but absolutely grateful to and loving the rival!

I had now got hold of the clue, with which I had as yet been merely toying. I must keep a watch at the Post-office, for I was satisfied, from his not having got a letter when he called that forenoon, he had one to get. He was clearly enough acquainted with the arrival of the mails, and I had only to be at my post next day at the same hour to get him into my embrace. I had, however, a little difficulty in my way, for it was clear enough that he had some premonition, from my apprehension of the boy, that I might be again about the Post-office; and he might send some other person for the letter. I required, therefore, to keep out of the way, and my plan was not to go into the clerks' room at first, but to edge about in the vestibule, till I saw him come up. I therefore took my stand in such a position that I could see him without being myself seen. I was aided in this by some collection of people.

Nor had I occupied my post long, till I saw him come in—more melancholy-looking than before; but then, was he not far away from his sweetheart in Woolwich? and the lover who was near him was one whom he not only did not know, but could not gratify by a return of his affections. He was now wary too,—at least he looked about him as if he feared the presence of him who had seized the thief,—and yet if he had had nothing to fear on his own account, he should have been glad to see him who had recovered the handkerchief; and here in the vestibule, and before going into the counter, there occurred a trifling circumstance that afforded me some amusement. I saw him take out another handkerchief where with he blew his nose, as if he had said to himself, as he sounded his horn, "I can blow my nose yet in spite of pickpockets;" and, what appeared to me to be curious, that handkerchief was of the same piece, being exactly the same pattern as the one he lost yesterday. Yes, and how minute suspicion becomes! It is not often that young men of his appearance buy *webs* of handkerchiefs; and I concluded, upon such whimsical evidence, that both handkerchiefs had been cut from the pawned piece. This notion amused me at least.

He then went in to the counter. I followed close up, and stood behind some people who were getting their letters or handing them over to be marked. He asked for the old address. It was that given by the Woolwich authorities. He got his letter, and I now expected that he would have walked away far enough from the Post-office. No; he was too keen to get into his widowed heart the words of love. He went out to the vestibule, and, looking about without seeing me, he opened the epistle and began to read. Being myself a suitor for his hand, and something more, I thought I had a right to see what was in my Woolwich rival's letter; so, as he was scanning it with all the attention of a lover, I quietly stood behind him, and, looking over his shoulder, began to read too,—"My dearest love," What a strange thing that love is! how independent of the moralities! Here it had flown on the wings of the wind three hundred miles to enfold (ay, and unfold) a thief, and cheer him in his solitude. But he soon observed that some one was standing behind him reading secrets.

"How dare you?" he cried, as he turned round; but my appearance stopped the rest of his sentence; for was I not the very man who had apprehended the boy, and might him?

"I can even dare more than that," I replied: "I can even ask your name and business."

He hesitated, and, as I thought, shook.

"But, in the first place," I continued, "give me that letter," taking it out of his hands. "This is *not* your name," looking to the back of it.

No answer.

"Is not your real name Milstead?"

"No; that is my name on the back of the letter. And why should it not be? I have this moment got it from the clerk."

"I know that, for I saw you get it."

"Then why doubt my word, and the name written there?"

"Because it is my trade to doubt, ay, and disbelieve, what I hear from certain people. I happen to know that your real name is Milstead; and if you have any desire to know whether my information comes from Wooler or Woolwich, you must go with me to the Police-office."

My melancholy friend now understood his position. A deadly paleness dashed his melancholy with increased solicitude; and, as I looked at him, I could not help feeling for one who, from the very arms of love, was transferred into the iron bonds of the law.

He submitted to his fate with a resignation that does not often belong to lovers, and walked with me to the office, where he was put to the question:—

"Where are you putting up here, Mr Milstead?"

"I deny that that is my name."

"Well, well, then Mr——." The name on the letter; it is not in my book.

"Nowhere. I am living in Glasgow, and come here only to receive my letters."

"Then, your luggage will be there?"

"Yes; anything I have."

"At what lodging-house there?"

"A hotel on the quay."

"Name?"

"Don't remember."

"Well," said I, "you and I will go to Glasgow together, and you will show me where you are putting up."

"I have no objections," he replied, with more confidence than I expected.

About an hour afterwards, my man and I were on the express train, going at the rate of forty miles an hour.

On arriving at the Broomielaw,—where he had said his hotel was,—he showed me the house, and there I ordered some refreshment for both of us. After which I went—leaving him in charge of a Glasgow officer I had picked up on the way—to the landlady of the hotel.

"What is the name of the young man I brought here just now?"

"Mr ——." The name on the letter again.

"Do you know anything about him?" I asked.

"Nothing. He came here some days ago, intending to set sail for America, and I understood he was waiting for a ship that is to sail to-morrow from Greenock."

"Has he any luggage?"

"A good deal," she replied; "but you know it is his, and I have no power over it."

"I am an Edinburgh officer," said I; "and I fancy that will be warrant enough for you."

"An officer! and is that gentle-looking, sorrowful young man a criminal?"

"That's what I want to know," said I; "and perhaps the luggage may help us."

"Well, I will take you to his bed-room; but stop," she continued, rather hesitatingly, "I have some money of his."

"How much?"

"Fifty sovereigns," said she.

"I will take that from you in the meantime," said I, "and then you will show me the luggage."

She went and got the money, counted it over to me, and I deposited it in my purse.

We then went into a bed-room, where she showed me his portmanteaus and trunks; a goodly stock for a voyage to America. I proceeded to take a partial survey, previous to a more perfect one when we arrived. My eye sought a certain pattern of a handkerchief, but I was for the present at least disappointed. I had now nothing to do but get my man and his baggage to the metropolis, and, accordingly, we again embarked.

While about half-way between Glasgow and Edinburgh, I noticed that my man was even more serious than ever. There was something passing in his mind; and every now and then he looked at me as if he had something very important to say to me. At length he whispered in my ear,—

"Mr M'Levy," for he had got my name from the Glasgow officer, "the only evidence upon which they can convict me in London is the articles and money you have got, I understand, from the landlady of the hotel."

"And enough, too," said I.

"Enough, and too much," he sighed; and after a few minutes' silence he continued, "I have been thinking, that if you are a man of any heart——"

"And conscience," I added, having a notion of what was coming.

"That if you were just to keep the money and the articles to yourself, and say nothing about it, I will say nothing."

"What more?"

"Why, then you might deliver me up to the London authorities, and I will not care much, because if they have nothing I have taken to bring against me, they cannot convict me."

"Very good," replied I; "but then I just fear that SOME ONE may convict me. Because you are acquainted with the devil, perhaps you think there is no God. No, no, my young friend, that's not my way of doing business. You forget I am a messenger of Justice, and you would bribe her."

He hung down his head on his breast, nor lifted it again during all the time of our journey.

On our arrival, I got him locked up; and perhaps my sorrow for my Jacques was a good deal modified by the recollection of his wish to tamper with my honesty, which had heretofore stood proof against all the temptations of glittering watches and diamond rings. The whole of my intercourse with this young man had been curious; but, I confess, there was one incident I was more concerned with than all the rest. Was it possible that I could find out, from his luggage, anything to satisfy me in regard to the mysterious hand-kerchief? I could have no peace till I should have gone over the whole; and this I did, but was again disappointed. I had next re-course to the young man himself, and, taking the article with me,

"You remember," said I, "the loss of your handkerchief at the Post-office?"

"Yes," said he; "a thief picked my pocket, and the letter fell out. I snatched up the letter."

"Which I have got," said I.

"Yes, but it did not tell you much."

"No, I confess it did not, because it is directed to your assumed address; but the handkerchief, it is that I wish to speak to."

"Well, what of that? I am in for it at any rate, and I don't care now what I say to you, if you will not use it against me."

"There is so much against you," said I, "that anything you may add will make no difference."

Some sighing again, which rather went to my heart, in spite of my recollection of the attempt to bribe me.

"Well, here is the handkerchief," said I; "and I wish you to tell me, only to gratify my own curiosity, whether that formed a part of the articles you carried off from the pawn-office?"

"Yes," said he, taking it into his hand; "it's one of a piece; and I had another of the same in my pocket when I was apprehended."

"Well," said I, "this is an extraordinary circumstance, and might teach you that there are higher powers than detective-officers. Upon that handkerchief, which was taken from you by the boy, I could have got you convicted, though I had not discovered another item of evidence against you."

"Most wonderful!" he ejaculated.

"Yes," said I; "but this is only one example out of many I have witnessed of such strange interpositions in my favour, that I have been often inclined to get on my knees in the street in reverent awe of that Eye which sees all, and of that Hand which can point Jus-tice to her object, while all the time we are thinking that we our-selves are the only agents."

The London officers came and took Milstead up for trial. I was present, and I need not say that the case was hollow against him, without my bit of miraculous discovery. Neither did I take any notice of the bribe, for I did not want to bear hardly against him. But the case was viewed as a serious breach of trust,—far worse, in one view, than robbery with force,—insomuch that an end of confidence between master and servant is an end to business—that very thing on which the greatness of Britain depends. He was sentenced to transportation for seven years.

The
Monkey-
Jacket

❖

If it be true, that which has been so often said, that we are, in our passage through life, all actors on the stage of the world, so must it be true that we are not always doomed to tragedy or melo-drama. No man, so far as I have been able to see, is limited or can limit himself to one part. Many who with their long faces and lugubrious speech seem cut out by nature for deep tragedy, can play broad farce very successfully, though it is not always they wish to be seen or get any applause for their performance. Even reverend gentlemen, I am sorry to say, do not always confine themselves to serious pieces; and certain it is, on the other hand, that many who seem to be formed for harlequins come off with great effect in tragedy, though often not with their own good will. If it were all quite voluntary, every one would know his cue and do it well, but it really is not that in most cases, and this makes the scene to an onlooker or philosopher the more queer, insomuch that we see every day broad grins changed into heavy chops, and hear roars of mirth dying away to rise in deep groans—tears of joy changed into those of grief, and so forth, and then t'other way as well. As for me, I play all kinds of parts, but then my feelings are merely of the sympathetic kind, seldom moved except in a professional way, so I have here an advantage. Even in my pity for criminals there is often mixed traits of enlivenment, and I have known, as I am now to relate, the gambols of a real monkey mixed with the griefs and sorrows of those who make worse than monkeys of themselves.

Some time in 1845 my good friend James Bell having got wearied of the routine of catching and being caught in turn—always the same thing over again—the rollicking and drinking

among depraved women, and then a long course of solitary meditation in the college of training at the Calton—merry and sad,
and sad and merry alternately—took a strange fancy into his head
that he might change all this into something like respectable uni-
formity, if not uniform respectability. But how was he to effect the
change? He couldn't get work. If he had gone to the Tron, as he
said to me, and bawled out, "A thief to let—what will you give for
him?—quite reformed, I assure you—reads his Bible, and tried
a revival once—five shillings a-week—who says?—the article's
at your service," he wouldn't have much chance of being employed. Then he couldn't work except as a labourer, and even as
such he could do little; for a steady shovel man requires both
perseverance and a certain some other thing for which we have
no name, but which in its result becomes apparent when you examine what he does by Hoppus. But why talk about a thief becoming a sweaty-browed, hard-palmed labourer? Bless you, the
thing is impossible! James Bell knew this, and even when he
wanted a change, didn't wish to work. He would be an easy gentleman, no longer disturbed by detectives; but how was this to be
effected in an old country like Great Britain?

Well, the plan adopted by him will show. James had had his
envy roused by these easy-going gentlemen who go about with an
organ and a monkey. It was doubtful, so various are tastes, if James
thought any creature higher or happier on earth than such a musical artist, actor, merrymaker, traveller, drawer of pennies, and free-
and-easy liver, always abroad during the day, and at night nobody
knows where. But, alas! every trade, except authorship and thieving, requires some capital. How was James to get the organ, the
monkey, and the velvet coat? Ay, but there's an old saying, that
nobody ever "bode for a silk gown but aye got a sleeve o't," and all
things need only a beginning. "The Little Warbler", it is said, was
the origin of a publishing firm in Edinburgh, which ultimately realised an income to the tune of ten thousand a-year, and James would
try a small beginning in his musical way. Lobby nobs did not wear
these nobby togas, velvet coats, and, after all, the monkey was of

greater importance. Now, there was a caravan in the Grassmarket, on the front boards of which a small homuncle, with a red jacket and a blue ribbon on his tail, played such gambols that he extorted the laughter of the youngsters of that part of the old town to an extent which induced James to believe that a fortune might be made out of him. If he could just get hold of that little hairy man he would give up thieving, and become a respectable member of society. But how was he to get him? The question was a difficult one, and he knew it by the very efforts he made to solve it as he stood in the front of the stage lights, and admired these wonderful evolutions, and meditated for hours together on the means whereby he could make the wonderful tumbler, posture-maker, and merry-andrew his own, without paying a penny for him, which penny he had not to pay.

But all James's cogitations came back to his professional notions, according as these did with a certain ancient maxim, that

> He should take who has the power,
> And he should keep who can.

There was nothing for it but to steal the little African and reduce him to slavery. If little things are great to little minds, what must great things be? And surely it couldn't be considered a small thing to steal an actor whose powers of laughter-compelling were equal to those of any comedian at the time on the boards, not excepting Sam Cowell himself, whom, indeed, in so far as regarded the pushing of the burlesque, he in some degree resembled. And steal him James did. Seizing an opportunity when the peripatetic inhabitants of the caravan had gone out to get some refreshment, after the late labours of the night, he contrived to open a door, to go in where the worn-out actor was reposing in well-earned sleep, and, seizing the unconscious victim, rolled him up in a piece of horse-cloth, to prevent scratching and screaming, and fairly kidnapped him. We are at no liberty to indulge in philanthropic reflections as to the feelings of the victim, only that he had feelings we must be pretty certain, when he found himself

> Forced from home and all its pleasures,
> To increase a stranger's treasures;

the last consideration being the only one that James thought of any importance. Neither need we try to fancy the surprise of the show-folk when they found him gone, on whom all their hopes of success in this world mainly depended.

Nor had James secured his prey without knowing where to take it—nowhere but to Lucky Gibb's in the Anchor Close, where there resided a number of the softer sex, yet not softer than the male who was to become their associate, and not inappropriately either, if we look to dispositions and habits, and compare the language of the one with the silence of the other. Nay, the comparison might be carried so as to be honourable to the new comer, insomuch as Mrs Gibb's female chimpanzees did not limit their actions to innocent frolic like their little relative, nor were they even true to their nearer kind, the ourangs, whom they cheated, seduced, and preyed upon, and small pity to these ourangs in particular.

There came next day the show-people to complain to us of the loss of their principal actor, a commodity in our way which you might suppose to be the most easily traced of all stolen things in the world. Not so fast. Jacko was not pawnable, neither could he be sold like a stolen nigger, nor was this disgrace intended to be put upon him. Then the women were so true to their human fancy, and so fond of the inhuman—we cannot say inhumane, for fear of ugly comparisons—that they kept him a kind of "lady's prisonier," so that I could not discover him any way. In addition to these difficul-ties there was a fair at Glasgow, where our showmen behoved to be, and as they left, no doubt with suitable feelings of sorrow, a day or two after, we were left without a proprietor to whom we could have restored the property.

Having made this auspicious beginning, the next part of James's stock-in-trade to be looked after was the organ. One might have thought that this was an article more easily got at than the live property, and yet, when you consider a little, you are apt to come to the conclusion, that to steal an organ-grinder's musical-box is a little more difficult than to get at Mr Jackson's. At least, so it appeared to James, an individual far better able to judge of both the difficulties and facilities of an adventure of this kind than you, I sincerely hope, can be, or with such as I before the eyes of your most ardent fancies ever will be. And then I might suggest the additional danger arising from the tell-tale nature of the article, as where it has been known to play a tune, such as "The Blue Bells of Scotland", too well known to the grinder himself or some one in his confidence. But an organ, though it could not be easily stolen, might be easily bought with stolen money, or the proceeds of stolen articles, and James saw in this direction his way to fortune. I fairly admit, that, in such calculations, his hope of being entirely independent of me was not consistent with his earlier aspirations, but he had it in his power, with the means of acting the gentleman always with him, of getting beyond my beat, away into the sunnier regions of England, or even into the vineyards of France, where he could feed himself and Jacko on grapes, and get the vintage-girls to dance a country-dance, with their castanets, to the strains of his organ.

That James did not consider the getting of the necessary funds a difficult affair turned out to be clear enough. Even I soon came to have evidence of this in the letter of Mr G——r from Polmont, which informed me that a shop in that place had been broken open, and a great quantity of soft goods taken therefrom, besides the contents of the till, amounting to five pounds. The robbers had gone thirds, and it was supposed they had proceeded with the booty to Edinburgh. The account of their persons led me to a suspicion, nothing more, that my hopeful organ-grinder was one, and, if I was right there, I could not be far wrong in regard to his associates, one of whom, James M'Kenzie, could not be absent when my James was in the way of doing what he called "good". But, mark, I didn't know all this time that James was working up to the organ and monkey pitch. That I ascertained afterwards, and, if I was right as to my man, I had just the present charge against him. With some notion that I had a right at least to these two, I set about seeking for these hard goods as well as the soft, and after some time began to suspect that they preferred Glasgow to their native city, perhaps because they didn't like me. Yet I persevered in the old way, trying every likely place, till at last I thought of Mrs Gibb, as good a customer to me as the lady of "The Cock and Trumpet". So one night I went to pay my respects—we never do use cards—and found the good lady in excellent spirits. I was introduced to her damsels, all collected in what she called her saloon, a barn-like room of considerable dimensions, plentifully lighted with gas, and having, you couldn't expect it in the Anchor Close, an old piano, worth thirty shillings, upon which some of her children, who aspired to be musical, could play a few notes, something like "Nid-noddin' ".

And upon this instrument one was accordingly trying to play amidst a roar of laughter which I could not for some time comprehend the meaning of, for the object of their mirth was in the midst of them.

"Well, lasses," said I, "what's all the fun?"

"It's Jacko," said Mrs Gibb by my side. "They've learned him to dance."

"Oh, my own Jacko!" said I to myself, getting on the instant as keen as any of them.

"It's Jim Bell's," cried Bell Ramsay, a small cricket of a girl, who, having a hold of the monkey, was dancing with him a kind of minuet to the notes of the rickety instrument.

"And who gave him that fine scarlet coat and silk sash?" said I.

"Jim, to be sure," cried another, a fat wench, Bess Brunton, who I knew was a favourite of Jim's.

"He's going to be an organ-grinder, James is," added the landlady, "and Jacko is to go about with him."

And the rest of her speech was lost in another roar, as Jacko, in remembrance of his former performances on the boards, got upon the back of Miss Ramsay, and began plucking her hair, screaming the while at the top of his voice.

"He's the merriest little devil in the world," continued Mrs Gibb.

"I don't know what we would do without him, and then he's such an amusement to the gentlemen."

"And the ladies, too," said I.

"Ay," cried the fat one, "Jacko is as good as a budge. He keeps us from 'the horrors.' "

"And that's not easily done," said I; "but where is James? does he live here?"

"Oh, you've nothing against him now?" cried the favourite again. "He's quite taken up now that he's to begin on the honest hook. He'll soon get the organ, and I'm to go with him to England."

"Oh, indeed!" said I, while my thoughts followed James further away. "You'll have a jolly time of it all three. James will play the organ, you the tambourine, and Jacko will dance."

"The very thing! and shan't we get the money?"

"But who made the jacket?" said I, getting so far professional as to presume, in the midst of so much fun, to think of the soft goods from Polmont.

"Me," replied the lusty one again.

"And you got the cloth from James?"

"Yes," and then "No," was the reply, as she began to gather her wits; "No, I bought it, for we wanted to make the little devil nobby. Stand up, you wretch, and let the gentleman see your scarlet coat."

And Jacko was immediately on the top of the piano, dancing in the way he no doubt did when with his old friends in the Grassmarket.

"Well," said I, "this is so funny a little imp, that I have taken a fancy to him as well as to his scarlet coat," and laying hold of him, while he screamed louder than the laugh of the girls, "I'll take him with me."

And to be sure the laugh was changed into a cry of perfect amazement as well as anger when they saw me inclined to carry off the very soul, as it seemed, of their "happy land".

"And what right?" cried she of the tambourine, who probably saw her hopes in as great jeopardy as Jacko.

"Never you mind that, lass," said I; "you will get Jim to comfort you in the absence of the monkey."

So I carried off my little man amidst as loud a shout of grief as was ever heard at an Irish wake; nor was it an easy matter, for he did not seem to like to leave his happy quarters among the women, who spoiled him; and I was not ill pleased when I got my prisoner— an innocent one in this case—deposited in a cell.

Now was my time for James. He would get information from his associate of the fate of the monkey,—and if it was true, as I suspected, that the red jacket was made by the girl out of some of the Polmont soft goods, he would see his danger, independently of the old charge for pug, and be off. I set a watch at the Anchor Close, though I did not expect much from a quarter whence he would get information of my seizure of his friend. I had better reasons for finding him somewhere else. At least I was now sure of him after knowing he was in Edinburgh. Being up to an old haunt of his in West Nicolson Street, I kept pacing there for nearly an entire day, and there accordingly, about four o'clock in the afternoon, I got my eye upon him. He was groggy, and in that devil-may-care state which comes on like a fever, after a great enterprise, such as the robbing of a shop.

"Well, Jim," said I, as I stood before him, "how goes?"

"Oh, very well!" with a grandish air; for while the whisky took away his fear, it had probably left his hope of becoming an independent musician and actor—"and how d'ye do?"

"Pretty well; only I have been sorry at not seeing you of late. What has become of you?"

"Oh, roughing it a bit here and there!" he replied.

"With your friend the monkey?" said I.

"Nothing to do with creatures of that kind. What the devil do you mean?"

"Well," said I, as my eye became fixed on a fine black satin cravat about his neck, which, from Mr G——r's letter, I had no doubt, had been once at Polmont, "since you're so saucy, I perhaps daren't ask where you got that elegant choker?"

"Oh, bought it, of course, you know," he replied, with really wonderful *sang froid* for one who knew himself to be so well known to me; "them things are got cheaper now, and I only need a scraper to be complete."

"Ay, and a velvet coat."

"Nothing of that kind," he replied.

"Or a red coat?" inquired I.

"No, don't like soldiering; never did."

"Except when you drill Jacko in the Anchor Close," said I, little nettled at his self sufficiency.

"Bosh and bunkum! quite out this time, my Lord Justice-Clerk."

"Now, master James Bell," said I, "are you positively certain you didn't get that satin cravat at Polmont?"

The never a train came to so dead a stand at that station as my fast passenger did now, when he saw that I had so much more serious a plea against him than that of the monkey. A blank look was my only answer, and I am not sure if he didn't get instantly sober on the premises.

"Come," said I, "I want to introduce you to an old friend."

"M'Kenzie?" he inquired, with a timid and suspicious look.

"Not at present," I replied; "you will meet him elsewhere. Another gentleman who wears a scarlet coat, the cloth of which also came from Polmont."

But even the mention of his facetious friend failed to remove his gloom, and as I saw I could get no more out of him, I took him to my quarters, where I was as good as my word, introducing him with appropriate ceremony to his old acquaintance, Jacko. But so far I had lost my pains, for they showed no affection towards each other, if they didn't exhibit manifest tokens of mutual hatred.

I had now my other friends to discover—M'Kenzie and his companion, whose name I don't find in my book. So I made my way again to the Anchor Close, where on the former occasion I had made a rather indifferent survey. I did not find what I wanted—the stolen property—but I found something that, perhaps, might suit my purpose as well. There was Bess sitting in a loose wrapper, and a fit of the horrors.

And now, my young ones still outside of these awful dens, and whom I cannot call *my* children, because you are not yet under my protection, just receive a little caution from me, who am so well able to give it. I have heard of some of you, very pretty too, and, therefore, the more in need of my suggestion, looking after these creatures—perhaps once your playmates—with their gaudy dresses, and faces whiter and redder than what they should be by nature, ay, my darlings, just as if you were envious of some elevation they have attained, and saying of one to your neighbour, (I have heard it said,) "How has *she* got so well on in the world? Set her up with her silks and satins and magenta ribbons, and I can scarcely get a coarse barege. How lucky some girls are!" Then you don't think, perhaps, that all this happiness is merely outside, and you don't, because you can't, see what is within. Well, when you get into your envious humour again, just mutter the two little words to your-selves—THE HORRORS. You may not comprehend their meaning altogether—I sincerely hope you never will—but you may depend upon it, it is something very terrible; ay, worse than hunger, and thirst, and cold, and nakedness—I was going to say death itself; and though I have not tried *that* yet, I know from what I have seen and heard of the closing agonies, that they do not equal the fearful and devilish tortures of "the horrors". Just keep this in mind when-ever you see any of these dressed-up and painted miserables, and there's no fear of you.

Well, my Bess was in a fit of the horrors, and that's the time to catch her kind, if you want to make anything of them.

"It's all up with Jim," said I. "I have caught him as well as Jacko, and you have now no chance of the organ and tambourine life."

"Oh! I can't speak to you," replied the poor girl, "until I get a glass."

"Not just now, Elizabeth, for then you know you would laugh me off in the old way, and you're not playing with the monkey now."

"We have been all miserable since the little devil left, and we want him back again. He kept us from the 'horrors', as I told you."

"A monkey?" said I.

"Ay, even a monkey. Didn't he make us laugh, and isn't that all we want when we get into the fit, and think of home and young days, and father and mother, and all that? Curse on the life we lead; we can't get quit of these thoughts; and then there's what's to become of us when used up?—the Infirmary—and something *yonder*, you know," pointing *down*. "Jacko kept all that ugly kind of thing away."

"So poor, so wretched a creature is woman, when she becomes the slave of vice," thought I; "not just pleased with a rattle and tickled with a straw, yet finding a relief from her misery in the unmeaning gambols of this uncouth animal."

"Well, what if I should give you him back, in the event of the showman not being found?"

"Let's have him," she replied; "but I'm to say nothing about Jim in exchange."

"Don't expect you, Bess; but I'll tell you what I want. You confessed that James gave you the monkey, and as it was stolen, I can take you up for resetting, and there's one twelve-month for you; then you admitted making the red coat for it out of cloth stolen from a shop in Polmont—there's other six for you."

"Oh, Jim told me nothing, and I'm not going to peach."

"Which you couldn't do if he told you 'nothing', you know."

"And won't, and there's an end on't."

"I don't want you to impeach James," I persevered. "I only want to know where M'Kenzie is, who was with him at the robbery. Remember the twelve and the six months."

"And you won't meddle with me, and you'll give us back Jacko?"

"I have said it."

"Well, M'Kenzie's a scurvy bilk, and I wish you may find him and the other too, at Mrs F——'s, in the Saltmarket of Glasgow; and now come away with a dram."

"Can't bribe, you know, Bess. Do you know where the stolen goods are?"

"No, except that M'Kenzie has the most of 'em; Jim is swearing at him, and that's all, and more than enough for me to say; but if it's all up with Jim and the organ, it needn't be all up with me too."

"No; and I thank you, Bess," said I. "I will do my best to keep you safe, and"—

"Give us back Jacko," she added, more cheerful.

"If I can," replied I.

And so I left Elizabeth, thinking, as I went along, upon the frivolity of the lives of these unfortunate creatures, who, cut off from all virtuous exercises of the mind and all true affections of the heart, endeavour to get quit of their griefs by means which to others would be only subjects of derision, contempt, and hatred. And this leads me to remark, that I think I have observed in most unfortunates a *want of mind.* I don't mean to say that they are devoid of a certain cleverness too, and some of the better of them may talk for a few moments with you pretty rationally; yet there is absent the mental balance, which enables people to weigh consequences, and keep on the broad end of the steel-yard in spite of temptation. I fear this throws more responsibility on the other sex, who have less of this infirmity than they are willing to admit.

Having got matters in so hopeful a train, for which I was indebted to pug, who in addition might have peached too, if he and his kind didn't know that man would set them to work if he knew they could speak, I wrote a letter to Mr G——r, wherein I told him I had secured James, and then directed him to the house in the Saltmarket, where, by writing to the Glasgow authorities, he would catch M'Kenzie and the other, as well as probably get a large portion of the property. I proceeded afterwards to get identified the fine satin cravat and the cloth of the scarlet jacket. I said nothing to Mr G——r of my medium of information; and I remember that he was filled with considerable wonderment how I could discover in Edinburgh, and point out so exactly, where he could find the burglars; and then I was entitled to my own laugh when I thought how much more his wonder would have been increased, and what a pleasant feeling of the ludicrous would have been excited, had he been informed of Bess and her favourite, and all the other details of the strange history of the projected organ scheme, wherein the three hopeful parties were to play their happy *rôles*.

Nor had Bess deceived me. The Glasgow authorities on receiving G——r's letter went direct to the house in the Saltmarket, and there, to be sure, found their two men, snug in their new lodgings, and as happy as liquid-fire thrown over callous hearts could make any of God's creatures who have renounced Him. A difficulty was likely to have occurred in this case, for the links of evidence were not very distinct. But it ultimately so turned out, that the one of the three, whose name, as I have said, has escaped me, became timid, not being a regular hand, and turned against those who had been his dear friends in prosperity, and kicked them in the old fashion, when Fortune reversed her wheel upon them. They were tried at Stirling, when Bell and M'Kenzie were sentenced to seven years' transportation. Who knows but that James might get his favourite scheme carried out after all, in a land where monkeys are more plentiful than men, and where there would be no necessity for stealing one to begin business with? I am speaking at random; I don't know much about the zoology of New South Wales. They have, they say, wonderful animals there, such as the duck-mole. It is said the country is *raw* yet, having come out of the sea long after the creation, and thus their animals are very imperfect, therefore it is possible there may be no monkeys—far more clever fellows, I suspect, than the natives. This defect I have done my best to supply, having sent out a good number of the real breed, but with a different object from those experimentalists who have been endeavouring to send out a breed of those innocent little thieves—the sparrows.

The
Coal-
Bunker

❖

A certain small critic once took it into his head to laugh at another critic for commencing a learned essay with the words, "We are all born idiots," and the reason of the chuckle, though on the wrong side, was evident enough; and yet, methinks, the wise saying might have had a tail, to the effect, "and many of us live and die idiots." At least I know that I have met many imbeciles,—ay, even of that absolute kind who will not be taught that pain is pain, so that I am obliged to differ with Solomon when he says that "experience teacheth fools." How many beacon flashes, with red streaks in them, have I not thrown out, amidst the darkness of crime, to keep my children off the quicksands and the shelving rocks, and the shipwrecks have been as numerous as ever! Have I not proved the Happy Land to be a hell, resounding with oaths, screams, and hysterical ravings, not the songs of angels, and yet case after case proved the truth of the wise saying?

Another flash of the beacon—with perhaps redder streaks—something of the old story, yet with a difference. On the second flat of the Happy Land there lived for some considerable time, in 1848, two young women, Isabella Marshall and Margaret Tait. Their den was of the common order,—the room and the hiding-hole, the bed, the fir-table, and two chairs, the teapot and cups, two or three broken plates, the bottle and glass, and so forth,—squalor everywhere, like the green mould which springs up the more when the sun of domestic comfort flies away at the sight of crime. Yes, the green mould on the once fair living temples; for let them wash, and scrub, and "scent up" as they pleased, and deck out in the stolen or thrice-redeemed finery, the snare of uncircumcised eyes and sensual hearts was only the covering of impurity. Yet how all this goes on and thrives. One might be tempted to say, that the lovers of "the beautiful"(?) are something like the gobemouches, who admire a little tang or *haut gout*. Look you, I use the *adjective* here, just with the proper amount of derision; for although the fairer of the two conjunct tenants of the den, Bella, was admired, no one could miss the Cain mark of the class. Don't you know it? Coarse snobs, with cassowary gizzards, might think they saw delicacy of skin and colour; while others, with a modicum of true refinement, would try to find another name—not easy, I confess—perhaps livid sickliness, reminding one of a decayed peony of the pale variety. Don't let us mention the faded lily. But what matters it, when the thing is patent to all but those who will not be taught by experience, just because there is nothing inside to respond to the touch of common sense. Yet withal there is something curious about Nature's manoeuvres, in fencing as she does to conceal the cancer-spots on her favourites, just as if she were so fond of her few beauties that she will cling to them to the last, supporting their charms even amidst the blight of vice. Of Margaret I must speak otherwise,—a strong, burly wench, with little to attract, but capital hands at a grip, or what is not exactly the same, a gripe, and a tilt where ferocity stands against self-preservation. The two were very well mated; for while the one could allure, the other could secure.

But as the den was incomplete without the hiding-hole, so neither was this copartnership of Marshall & Co. perfect without the indispensable "bully"; for though Margaret could do wonders in her way, she could derive little aid from the delicate Isabella. So James Kidd, a stout young fellow, the Fancy of both, who apportioned his protection and favour between them according as they supplied him with money, was the chosen partner,—a fellow who, in such a connexion and conspiracy, had found an attraction which tore him from his home and his mother, whose heart he had broken. Nor is it easy otherwise to form a proper estimate of this species of ruffian, pouncing from a hole on a man whose powers of resistance he does not know. He must close in a struggle, which, though never intended to be deadly on his part, may become so, by a resistance or counter attack more powerful than his own. All this he must do in the very heart of a populous city, and in a large house of many flats, where he can count upon no more than the hush of other fiends, who may screen, though they will take no hand in another's business. It is in such a scene, enacted in a close room, sometimes with the light extinguished, and the actors doing their work in the dark, that we can form an adequate idea of the true *furor* of robbery. Even a listener at the door would hear only the bodily contortions— the deep breathing—the muttered vengeance—all a deep bass to the stifled treble of a woman's passion grasping at gold. I have known of two such conflicts going on in this "Happy Land" at the same moment,—the great scenes being illustrated the while by orgies in the other dens, the laughter from which drowned the dull sounds of the conflicts.

In the particular conspiracy I am now to relate, the scheme of attack was different from what was usually followed, as you will understand when I introduce Mr —— of ——; and you have only at present to keep in mind the general way of "doing" the victims:- the spring-out of the concealed bully—the seizure of his object— the assistant women rifling and robbing in the still flickering light— the sudden disappearance of the principal actor, which aids the blasphemous oaths of the subordinates that they know nothing of him, while it leaves the conversational winding-up to those whose conversational powers are so seldom at fault.

On a certain night of the cold month of December, the delicate Isabella, dressed in the usual mackerel-bait, only a little subdued by the soft muff and boa, so suggestive of softness and delicacy in the wearer, went out on her mission of love, leaving Kidd and Margaret to await the bringing in of the prey. Nor was it long before she encountered the sympathetic Mr —— from Cumberland, who could make pleasure wait on business—just as a pretty handmaiden who comes and goes, and goes and comes. Oh yes, seldom coy, that faithful helpmate of anxious hearts—always everywhere and yet nowhere, turning her face and disappearing to return again. Then why shouldn't sympathy for a tender creature, exposed to a December chill, help the sympathy due to himself? He would not prey on that tenderness—only purchase a little pleasure with money that would nurse the seller in that land of bliss, where Justice would see to a fair bargain, Love filling the scales with hearts. So Mr —— would go with Isabella; all in the old way—respectable house—matronly mistress. Why, it would even be a duty to warm with a glass of generous spirits so gentle a creature. Up the North Bridge, and down the High Street—a sudden stand at the foot of the stair of the Happy Land. Mr —— did not think there was much promise of pleasure in that dark old region of sin, and he would be off and leave her who required so much sympathy from hard-hearted man. But Mr —— was a man of feeling notwithstanding, and how could he resist an appeal to his heart by one who asked no more than his arm up the star? Nor did he. With Isabella receiving the proffered support, he mounted the stair. They entered the dingy lobby, and came to a door. The gentle knock, not to disturb the decent woman, and Margaret,

—"who knew the meaning of the same,"

opened, but not until Kidd had got into the closet.

Whether it was that our gentleman had heard some noise of a retreat, or that he had had his prior doubts confirmed by the smoky appearance of the den, I cannot tell, but certain it is that the startled lover stopped again.

"No, I have seen enough," he cried, and was retreating, when Margaret, laying hold of him, pulled him in by main force.

"Away so soon," she cried, laughing, while yet retaining her masculine grasp, "and not even bid us good night?"

"Or offer us a glass," added the gentle Bella. "Surely two women can't harm a man!"

But Mr ——, who had felt, and was feeling, the tenderness of Margaret's love embrace, was perhaps more dissatisfied than ever, and hearing the click of the bolt under Isabella's stealthy hand got more resolute. Out goes the light, and now commenced one of those struggles for which the Happy Land was so famous. Another man, on thus finding himself encaged, and so suddenly deprived of light, might have succumbed to fear; but our hero was not of the timid order, who can enjoy love and be dead to the trump of war. Not even when he heard the spring of Kidd, as he bounced from his cell, did he think of yielding, but, by a strong effort throwing off the women, he made towards the door. He had even succeeded so far as to search for the lock, but found, to his dismay, that the key had been taken out. On turning round he was immediately in the grasp of Kidd, with the women hanging upon him. And now was the real conflict; all the contortions—the deep breathings from the oppressed lungs— the thumps on the sides of the room—but not a word of speech, only smothered mutterings and oaths ground between the teeth.

The effort on the part of the assailants was to get the gentleman on his back on the floor; nor could this issue be prolonged for many minutes, with a force of three arrayed against one. Yet the attempt failed more than once, an interval being occupied by a cry for help, shouted at the top of his voice, and responded to by an orgie-laugh from the further end of the lobby, and some suppressed mirth at the back of the door, as if some creatures of human shape were there, in the full enjoyment of what was likely to be their own game at another time. As confessed by Mr ——— afterwards, this evidence of how completely he was, as it were, doubly or trebly caged, struck him with more dismay than even the extinguishing of the light or the bound of Kidd from his recess. The idea took hold of him that he was to be murdered, and though under this energy, inspired by the love of life, the increased strain brought up in his enemies by his now desperate resistance laid him flat on his back, with such force that his head dirled to the brain.

The remaining part of the process was easy—the gold watch pulled out of his pocket, the click of the bolt, and Kidd was gone.

"Catch the thief!" cried Margaret, with just enough of force as to reach the ears of the poor victim, as he lay stunned with the knock on the head, and almost exhausted by the struggle.

"He's gone," added the gentle Isabella.

"Who is gone?" said Mr ———, as he looked up in the now lighted room.

"Why, the d——d villain who has taken your watch," replied Margaret.

"An accomplice," groaned the victim, as he attempted to rise.

"It's a lie, sir," replied Margaret again, with increased fury, as she breathed fast from her exertions. "The fellow lives ben in the other room, and this is not the first time he has played us a trick of the same kind; but he'll be hanged same day."

"Yes, and the sooner the better," joined Isabella.

"Come, we cannot help it. There's no use following him.

Give us a dram for defending you."

"Ay, for saving your life," added her neighbour; "for we know he would have murdered you."

"I felt *your* hand on my throat," cried Mr ——.

"Bob's, you mean," was the answer. "He has a hand like a woman, and yet it would choke a tiger."

"I felt all your *six* hands on me," roared he, unable to stand even this transparent dodge.

"How could we know you from him in the dark?" cried Margaret. "We intended to pull him off; and that's our thanks, and you'll not even give us a 'budge,' but accuse two innocent girls for being robbers."

"Oh, it's the way with them all," added Isabella. "They first ruin us, and then charge us with theft; but we deserve it, don't we, for trusting their lying words."

"Liars and thieves, one and all of you," replied the gentleman. "You know you inveigled me here to be robbed by your bully. That watch cost me £20."

"Well, then," said Margaret, "give us £5—you have money about you somewhere—and we'll tell you where you will catch him."

"Worse and worse," ejaculated Mr ——; "but what am I doing here?" he added, as he for the first time, after recovering from his stupor, bethought himself of following the thief; and gathering up his hat, and arranging his torn garments, he made for the door.

"Not till you pay us for saving your life," said Margaret, as she stood between him and the door, with the intention, no doubt, merely of gaining time for Kidd.

And so, to be sure, she made only a faint effort to hold him back, and he, pulling open the door, rushed out into the dark passage, saluted as he disappeared by the hoarse laugh of the women, and, as he thought, some other indications of the same kind from the sympathisers further ben. Glad to get off a living man, but yet not inclined to give up as lost his valuable property, he half walked and half tumbled down the stair of this, to him, most *unhappy* land; nor did he stop till he was in my presence in the Office. A few words, uttered with much difficulty, very soon satisfied me that he was one of a host who had been turned away from the Happy Land with less ceremony than "Frau Schnipps," on an occasion not altogether similar.

"Wait there," said I," I will bring up the women in the first place."

"Oh, you know them?" said he.

"Yes, about as well as you, sir."

"And that's too well," said he, with something like a heave of the chest.

"Bell Marshall and Margaret Tait," said I; "but they haven't the watch, and I know they will say they were helping you. The man is my object."

So leaving him, and taking with me two constables, I went to the scene. As I expected, I found the girls. Two or three of the children of the Happy Land were with them, all engaged in drinking and laughing, no doubt at the excellent drama that had just ended, and upon which they thought that the green curtain had been drawn for ever, for it is not very often that the slain hero makes his appearance again at our Office; and there can be no question that sometimes it is as prudent to pocket shame as it is to put a gold sovereign into your purse, with the difference, that while the one ought to remain, the other should come out for the benefit of society. I was not expected, and was accordingly greeted with the honour of perfect silence.

"The old game, my lasses," said I, as I beckoned to the others to get off, which they very soon did, growling as they went along the passage; "where is the gentleman's watch?"

"Search, and answer for yourself," replied Margaret.

"The man has it."

"What man?"

"How should we know? He came *in* upon us; we did our best to save the gentleman, and the scurvy dog wouldn't give us a penny to buy pins."

"Came *out*, you mean," said I; "the old story, 'the great unknown.' Yet I think I know him."

Just as I was speaking, I felt some small object under my foot, and stooping down found a small gold watch-key. The women looked sharp to try and find out what I had picked up and put into my pocket, but they said nothing, neither did I.

"Come," said I. "The gentleman is in the Office, and wishes to thank you for trying to save his life."

"Umph, and true, by ——," said the reprobate.

"A terrible fellow this 'unknown,'" said I, rather by way of amusing myself as they were getting equipped. "Don't pare your nails, for I intend to introduce him to you."

And proceeding to make a search, which I knew would be attended by no greater result than a mocking laugh from my lasses, I was forced to be content with my small recovery of the gold key.

I marched them up to quarters where they had been before. It was too late that night to go after Kidd. I was sure enough of him, and an early catch was of no use as regards the recovery of the watch, which I knew he would not carry with him a moment longer than he could find a hiding-place for it, and that he would find far more readily than one for himself.

Next morning some of the constables, who knew where Kidd's mother lived in the Pleasance, thought very wisely they might help me in their way by searching the house. This they accordingly did before I was well out of bed; but their report was unfavourable. He was not in the house, and the mother denied all knowledge of her worthless son. I have often had reports of this kind made to me before, but I have been always fond of making my own searches. So away I went to do the work over again; but, to say the truth, I had little hope. It was as early as nine.

"I want to know where James is," said I, as I entered the little shop.

"God bless me," said she, with wondering eyes, "more policemen! why the men are scarcely awa'. They searched the hail house, and found naebody. Am I no enough tormented and heartbroken wi' a neer-do-weel son, but I maun be treated as his keeper, whether I hae him or no, and my house searched by man after man, as if I mysel' were a breaker of the laws."

"I know you are not a breaker of the laws, Mrs Kidd," replied I, calmly, "and that's the very reason why you should even cheerfully allow an officer to go through your house. I am not in the habit of stealing, and, besides, I wish you to go along with me."

"But there's nae occasion," was the reply. "Have I no tauld ye your men are scarcely out o' the house, and lang and sair they searched. It's no that I fear aught, nor the trouble either, but it's the nonsense."

"I will put up with the nonsense," said I.

"Maun I tell you a third time," said she, with increased firmness, "that my house has been searched by twa men, wi' twa een each, this morning already?"

"Then two eyes more can do the less harm?" replied I, with a quiet pertinacity at least equal to her own, especially, and no doubt a consequence of, the said pertinacity on her part, which appeared to me somewhat more than was required, according to her own theory.

"Weel, een here or een there, there's naebody in my house, and what's the use of our paying for your men, when you have nae faith in them ony mair than in me?"

An adroit reply, but somehow the more she said the more I thought, only in a different direction. I had dallied myself into suspicion, and had little time to spare.

"Come," said I, "let us end this; but I have consideration. I don't want to trouble you to go up stairs with me."

"I've been up already with the men," she persisted, "and really I'm no just pleased to hae my word doubted. I'm no a policeman, and I've aye thought that when a man doesna believe me, he thinks me a leer. Just gae your wa's, and be sure there's nae James Kidd in my house."

"Well," replied I, getting impatient, "I must just step up myself."

"Weel," was the tardy reply, "a wilfu' man maun hae his ain way. Come awa', and ye'll see what you'll mak o't."

And leading the way very reluctantly, she preceded me up to the little flat. I entered the kitchen, and began to peer about as carelessly to appearance as usual; but I confess I saw nothing which could lead me to suspect that there was any human being there except Mrs Kidd and myself; and she did not seem inclined to condole with me in my disappointment, though I could see, too, that she abstained from showing any triumph in my discomfiture.

"You see how little harm my survey is doing you," said I. "It is even pleasant work."

"It's no to me, whatever it may be to you," said she. "You are searching for my son, and isn't that enough for the heart of a mother? You're maybe no a father, and canna ken thae things. Ay, it's sair to hae the heart broken by the hands that should hae comforted it and bound it up. It's the turning back o' the yearning that braks it; but now I fancy ye're satisfied James is no here."

And I felt for the poor woman. I had the parlour to look through; but as the sounds of her grief fell on my ear, I stood musing a little, and when the mind is occupied, the eye trifles, and mine trifled, as well as did my foot, as I used it in kicking away a bit of coal, a "churl" as we call it, that lay before me. At the same instant my eye caught the heap of coals in the corner, and two thoughts came into my head—first, why the coals should be in *that* place; and secondly, why the "churl" should be in *this* place. It had not come there where it lay by having been dropped, because it was not in the line to the fire, and then it was at the edge of a little door which had escaped my notice; or rather, I should say, it was so small an affair, without sneck or lock-handle, that I thought it a mere cup-board. Again, why was the "churl" so situated as if it had come out of the small recess? And once more, why was the cupboard without a projection whereby it could be opened? Ah, well, how the mind will work even when it is playing.

"What place is this?" said I.

"Oh, a little cupboard," said Mrs Kidd; "just a place for cups and saucers."

"Which you use every day?"

"Every day."

"And yet there is no sneck-handle, whereby you can get in when you are maybe in a hurry for a cup of tea?"

No answer from poor Mrs Kidd, and the thought came that the coals in the corner were surely out of place, in a little tidy house; and just mark how that kind of natural logic works.

"I should just like to look in."

"And what would be the use? Hae ye never seen a number o' marrowless cups and saucers?"

And maybe something even more marrowless, thought I, as, tak-ing out a penknife and inserting it in a small slit, something like that of a check lock, I opened the door, and there, lying in a hole—the veritable bunker— was my friend of the Happy Land, extended on a small mattress. On this exposure, the poor mother covered her face with her hands and sobbed hysterically.

"The last o't," she said, in a voice broken by sobs. "The lang train o' griefs a' frae whaur there should hae come comfort and help is wound up. I hide and conceal nae mair, and what signified my hiding when God saw through a'. Tak him, sir; and may ye mak o' him a better man to his brither-man, than he has been a son to me."

"Has he given you a watch?" said I, in the expectation of prof-iting by what I considered to be a breaking down.

"No," she replied, "I have never had ony o' his secrets, nor for a lang time has he been near me, except when he wanted meat. His wild ways are best kenned to himsel', but I fear women and drink have been his ruin."

"Rise, James," said I," and give me the watch you robbed the gentleman of last night in the Happy Land."

"I deny it," replied the incorrigible rogue, as he rose slowly, cursing between his teeth.

I searched the house, but the watch was never recovered. The three were brought to the High Court. It was a difficult case, in consequence of the darkness of the scene, which prevented recognition of Kidd; but a strange circumstance supplied the want. Mr —— could swear that Kidd had a large hard wart upon the right hand—the rough pressure of which in his neck had pained him so as to leave an impression on his mind. The wart was found still upon the thumb. Then the watch-key served its purpose, and it was found that Kidd was the daily associate of the women. They were each transported for fourteen years.

The
Mustard-
Blister

❖

I believe that if any one were to look back upon his past life for the purpose of tracing out the most curious parts of it, he would find that they originated in the work of my old lady, Chance, and which is nothing more than something occurring just at the moment when it is unlooked for, but, being taken advantage of, turns out to be important. The great secret is to be able to seize the advantage, and this, as concerns my kind of work, lies in something like natural reasoning. If there's anything out of the ordinary fitness of things, I begin to try to find out why it should be so. Books and learning don't help a man here. I have sometimes thought they rather work against him, and hence it is that we find so many illiterate people rise up to be great and wealthy. Ay, but they can also be clever in a bad way; so with our thieves; but I have this consolation, that if their mother-wit has done a great deal for them, mine has also to their cost done something for me. I will give you a case.

In 1845, there were almost daily occurring cases of robbery from larders in the New Town, and, what was more extraordinary, the accounts all tallied as to the fact that the thieves were exceedingly dainty. It was only the fine pieces of meat that would please them—large joints and legs of mutton—nor did they seem to care for cold meat, in some instances leaving it, as if they were above that kind of food. Of course, I had my ordinary professional reasons for being active in endeavouring to lay hold of these burglars, who seemed to be so envious of the good things of their neighbours, but I confess to the weakness of having had a little of that same feeling in regard to them. I was not easy under the notion that any of my children should be thus living at hack and manger in so very much more luxurious a manner than myself, and felt a great desire to show them the difference between these hot joints and the fare I am in the habit of providing for them.

But how was I to get hold of them? Who could trace a leg of mutton after it was cut down and eaten? No wee pawns for joints or beefsteaks, and then the omnivorous gentry are generally so hungry that they could not afford, however epicurean, to lay past, to get tender and high-flavoured, a gigot of wether mutton or piece of venison. Then as to catching red-hand, that was out of the question, for upon inquiry it was found that the thieves never tried a larder a second time. I could, in short, make no discovery, and I was more uncomfortable under my want of success than I generally am, insomuch that my cooks were not only angry at losing their joints, but driven into a passion at the gentry's dinners being spolit by the disappearance on the previous night of some "old leg" which had been kept a fortnight for the very occasion, and which could not be supplied by the butcher. Their honour was at stake, and we all know what the honour of a *cuisinière* amounts to when the same is calculated by the dripping lips of a *gobemouche.* I have caught "old legs," which, like Madeira, had been sent over the sea to improve, and have found them improved in the contrary way, but here my "old legs" defied me.

I had given up hope, and my angry cooks were left to look better after the joints that were to be used in future, when one night I happened to go into the shop of Mr M'Dougal at the foot of the High Street. There were several people in the shop, and I stood back, not to avoid the gaze of Mrs Biddy Riddel of the Fountain Close, (her maiden name was O'Neil), who didn't look for me, and didn't see me, for, in truth, I was after no game that evening, but merely to avoid interfering with the customers. Now was Biddy's turn to be served.

"Half an ounce ov good tay—an ounce ov sugar—and an ounce ov raal Durham musthard," said she.

The purchase struck me as being singular, and I'm sure the grocer was of the same opinion. I was perfectly aware that she was of the class of the half-ounce-of-tea-and-glass-of-whisky buyers, and if she had asked the whisky I would have considered the purchase as quite in the ordinary way, but the "raal Durham" was quite another thing, and I could account for it nohow.

I saw that the grocer had looked at Biddy when she asked the mustard, just as if he felt inclined to ask what she was to do with so large a quantity, nay, any quantity, however small, but he proceeded without saying a word to tie up the tea and the sugar, then, coming to the third article,

"Did you say an ounce of mustard, Mrs Riddel?"

"Ay, raal Durham."

"Why, that will go a far way with you," said Mr M'Dougal, as he looked over to me, and laughed—a kind of interference with the rights of trade that Biddy did not seem to relish.

"Wid me?" she said; "and why wid me? Shure, couldn't I buy a pound ov it if I chose?"

"And most happy would I be to sell it to you," was the reply.

"Ay, and I may need a pound ov it too," she continued, "if it doesn't plase the Lord to be kinder to me; for hasn't Willie caught a terrible cowld, and amn't I to put a blisther on his throat this blissid night?"

"Ah, that's another thing, Mrs Riddel. I'm sorry for William. His trade of chimney-sweeping takes him early out in the cold mornings."

"And shure it does," she replied; "but the never a bit less shame to ye to think I was to ate musthard like honey and the devil a bit ov salt mate to take wid it."

"I am sorry for the mistake," said the grocer, as he rolled up the small packet, and Biddy laid down the pence.

"And so you may," added she, not altogether reconciled; "and, what's more, have I not as good a right to a piece of salt bacon as the gintry?"

And not contented yet without the parting salute—

"And ye don't know yet that we kept pigs at home, at Ballynagh; ay, an' they more than paid the rint; and, what's more, bedad, we didn't need to tie the bit ov bacon to the ind ov the string and swallow it, and thin pull it out agin."

"I believe it, Mrs Riddel," said the grocer. And then the last words came—

"And what's more, it wasn't straiked wid a hunger and a burst, like your gintry's. Just purty white and red where it should be; and we had musthard, too, galore, when we wanted it. Shure, and I've settled your penn'orth, anyhow."

And so she had; for as she went grandly away, carrying in her hand her half-ounce of tea, and in her head the honour of Ballynagh, Mr M'Dougal looked as if he had committed an error in joking as he had done on the wants of the poor.

"You've raised the lady's dander," said I.

"Which I shouldn't have done," said he, "for her penny is as good to me as another's; and then she needs the mustard for the *outside* of her son's throat, not the *in*."

To which sentiment I agreed, even with a little sympathy for the feelings of a mother, whose penny for a blister for her son's throat was just the tribute which she could ill spare paid from a mother's affection to old Æsculapius. I confess to having been somewhat amused by Biddy's Irish vindication of the rights of her family, but having been merely amused, the interlude passed out of my mind— so completely so, that by the next morning I was thinking of something very different from Mrs Riddel and her invalid son, Willie, with the sore throat.

Next day I was passing the mouth of the Fountain Close, and whom did I see standing there, with a pipe in his mouth, but Bill himself, arrayed in his suit of black, with face of the same, indicating that he had been at work in the morning? He was quite well known to me, and from a circumstance which will appear ludicrous. I had occasion at one time to separate him from a baker with whom he had quarrelled, and with whom, also, he had fought so long that the two had so mixed colours that you couldn't have told which was the man of the oven or the man of the chimney; but the truth is, that he had more to answer for than thrashing a baker, for he was an old offender in another way, where he took without giving something more than dust. Of course it was a mystery to me how he had so soon recovered from his sore throat, and the effects of the "raal Durham."

"Well, Bill, how's your throat, lad?" said I, going up to him.

"My throat?" replied he; "nothing's wrong with it—never had a sore throat in my life."

"Except once," said I.

"When?"

"When I took you by it rather roughly," said I.

"Unpleasant recollection," said the rogue. "Don't wish it mentioned. Steady now,—nothing but lum-sweeping and small pay."

"And no mustard-poultice last night?"

"Mustard-poultice? Strange question! never had a mustard-poultice in my life."

"Quite sure? let me see your throat."

"More sure than I am that you're not gibing a poor fellow," replied he, pulling down his neckcloth. "I don't belong to you now, so be off unless you want me to sweep your vent for sixpence—cheap, as things go, and I'll leave you the soot to hide your shame for what you did to me yon time."

Well, I took the joke, and really I had no reason in the world for doubting his word as to either the throat or the blister, but I confess I was startled, and couldn't account for the discrepancy between the story of the lady of Ballynagh and that of her son. Things were out of their natural fitness; and there was some explanation required to bring them into conformity with it and themselves. What that explanatory thing was I couldn't tell, and so I walked into the grocer's.

"Why," said I, "Biddy Riddel's black darling has no sore throat, after all, he is standing at the close-head quite well, with his throat, which I have seen, as black as soot.

"Strange enough," said he.

"Have you sold her any ham of late?' said I, after musing a little.

"Too poor for that," he replied; "all goes for whisky, and Biddy's half-ounces of tea, with, no doubt, a bit of coarse meat occasionally, to which an ounce of Durham would, of course, be out of the question."

"Did she ever buy from you any mustard before?" I inquired again.

"Why, now when I recollect, yes," replied he. "About a week ago she had an ounce. I had really forgotten that, when last night I touched her on a tender part."

With my additional information I left the shop, meditating as I went up the High Street on the strangeness of the affair, small though it was—for a little animal is just as curious in its organization as a big one, and I've heard of some great man who lost his eyesight by peering too closely into these small articles of nature's workmanship. I didn't intend to lose mine, and yet I couldn't give over thinking, though it is just as sure as death that I saw no connexion between what I had heard noticed and the larder affair, neither then nor afterwards, during the day. Besides, another business took the subject out of my head, so that I thought no more of it.

Next morning, as I was proceeding to the Office, my attention was again called to the mystery of the mustard-blister, by encountering the lady of Ballynagh carrying a stoup of water from the Fountain Well, and I couldn't resist a few words as I passed.

"Well, Mrs Riddel," said I, with true official gravity, "how is your darling's throat after the blister?"

"And it's you that has the impidence to ask it?" replied she; "are you a docthor?"

"Yes, I sometimes try to mend people when they're *bad*."

"To kill them, you mane, and the heart ov many a dacent widdow besides," was the reply.

"But I didn't make Bill's throat sore this time."

"No more ye did; but small thanks to ye, for wouldn't ye hang him, if yez could? and, shure, to hang a man wid the proud flesh in his throat would be a mighty plaisant thinng to the likes ov ye; and didn't I look down it wid me own eyes?"

"But Bill says he never had a sore throat in his life."

"And isn't that becase he's so bowld a boy?" replied she. "He never complains, becase he knows it would hurt me; but is that any raison I shouldn't blisther him when he's ill? And didn't I know he was ill when he could only spake like a choking dog, and couldn't for the life ov him take a cup of tay or ate a bit ov bread?"

And taking up her pitcher, she hurried away, leaving me as much in the dark as ever on this great subject, destined to become so much greater before even that day was done, but not by any exertions of mine, for as yet I could see nothing in it beyond the fact that there was some incident required to be known to bring out the fitness of things. Nor was it long before I got satisfaction. The day was a strolling one with me, more a look-out for "old legs" than a pursuit after new ones, and for some reason which I don't now recollect, I was in Hanover Street, along which I had got (it was now dark) a short way when I observed a sweep coming along with a jolly leg of mutton in his hand. We are sometimes blamed for being somewhat curious in our inquiries into the nature of carried parcels, but here there was so much of the real unfitness of things that I might, I though, be justified in my curiosity—all the more, too, when I discovered that the proprietor or carrier was my friend of the sore throat.

"Where got you the leg of mutton, Bill?" inquired I, as I stood before him, and stopped his quick pace, intended to be much quicker the moment he saw me.

"The leg of mutton?" replied he, taken aback.

"Yes," said I, "just the leg of mutton. It is so seldom you have a thing of that kind about you that I feel curious to know."

"You might as well ask that gentleman where he got his umbrella or his coat," was the cool reply.

"Not just the same," said I; "but I do not choose to point out the difference. Where got you it?"

"Bought it to be sure, and that's enough for you."

"Quite enough," said I, "if you did buy it, and I confess you have a good taste. A better leg I haven't seen for a long time. An 'old leg' too, and just kept long enough to be tender. Who's your butcher?"

"What's that to you?"

"Perhaps I might fancy one the same," said I; for I felt inclined to play a little as the idea of the mustard began to tickle my brain and make me merry. "I might even fancy that one and offer a premium upon it."

"What premium?" he said, perhaps not knowing very well what to say.

"Perhaps sixty days and 'skeely' without a drop of mustard."

The word operated like a charm on my sooty epicure, but he didn't seem to understand it any way, looking into my face inquisitively, and no doubt remembering the conversation about the blister without being able to connect the two things, for doubtless his mother had told him nothing of his sore throat and of the remedy.

"Come," said I, "there are just two ways. You take me to the butcher's shop or I take you to mine."

Bill was too sensible a fellow not to see, even without the quickening of the blister, that it was all up with him, and so accordingly, carrying his leg of mutton, he accompanied me very quietly to the Office, where I deposited him and his burden. I now examined the leg with the view of endeavouring to ascertain whether it might be identified, for I was here in the position I was in that morning I had so much difficulty about my booty in the Cock and Trumpet. But I soon discovered what I thought might serve my purpose, and, telling the lieutenant to take care not to allow the leg to be handled, I took my way to the Fountain Close, where I found my proud lady of Ballynagh sitting at her ease, no doubt expecting her son in by and by, or at least before supper, which supper he would doubtless bring in himself, she providing the mustard.

"I'm just here again," said I, as I opened the door and went in.

"Ay, always shoving in your nose where you've no more right to be than in heaven, where you'll never have any right at all," replied she. "'What wid me now?"

"I just want to know, Mrs Riddel, what you did with the ounce of mustard you bought two nights ago at Mr M'Dougal's?"

"The musthard?" she exclaimed, at the top of her voice.

"Just the 'raal Durham.'"

"The raal Durham! and what should I do wid it but make a blisther for Bill's throat, as I towld ye before, and tell ye agin?"

"And yet here is the most of it in this cup, ready made for supper," said I, as I took from the old cupboard the article and held it before her.

"And was I to use it all at wunst for a blisther, d'ye think, ye mighty docthor M'Lavy?" said she, with something of her usual greatness; "and isn't his throat sore and won't he naid the rest ov it this very night?"

"Then what will become of this fine piece of salt beef?" said I, as I pulled out of the same recess the article which appeared so strange in a small hovel, with two chairs and a table, and scarcely a bit of furniture besides. "You must reserve a little for it?"

"And who gave ye the power to spake about my mate, and ask whether I ate musthard to it or not? Isn't it me own?"

"That's just what I want to know," said I, as I took out my handkerchief to roll it up in.

"And who knows that better than the woman who bought it, and salted it, ay, and put saltpatre upon it, and hung it, and boiled it?"

"And told me that the mustard was for her son's throat," said I.

"Ay, and the thruth, too, every word ov it."

"Well, I'm going to take the beef to the Police Office, where Bill is," said I; "I will leave you the mustard."

"If you are going to be a thaif, take it altogether," cried, "and may the devil blister your throat before you try to ate what belongs to a poor widdow! And you've ta'en up the boy agin, have yez?"

"Yes".

"For stailing his own mate?"

"And if you are not quiet," said I, "I will return and take up you for helping him to eat it."

"And that would just make the right ind ov it, you murtherin' spoiler ov widdows and orphans."

And now that she had begun to abuse me I might get more of her "good words" than I wanted, so I left her, hearing, as I went down stairs, as many of the malisons as would have served, if they had been blessings, for the contents of all the rifled larders.

I had nearly got to the Office when a cook from Inverleith Terrace came and reported the theft of a leg of mutton. I was now pretty certain I had not overstepped my duty in apprehending Bill, but the difficulty remained as to the identification.

"Would you know your leg if you saw it?" inquired I.

"As easily as I would know my own, if it were cut off," she replied, with a grim smile.

"Is that it, then?" said I, as I showed her the article.

"The very leg," said she. "There's. the wether mark and the snip off the tail, to show me which I was to use first, and tomorrow is the great dinner day."

"I was trusting to the string," said I, as I held within my hand the piece by which the leg had been hung on the hook.

"And so you might," replied she, "for it is a piece of an old window cord which was lying on the dresser, and the rest of it is still in the kitchen."

"Is that it?"

"The very bit; I tied it with my own hands. But how in the name of all that's wonderful, has the leg found its way here before me?"

"Never you mind that," said I. "You will be able to swear to the article?"

"Ay; but what am I to do for the dinner?"

"Why," said I," you could scarcely serve up to your master and his guests a leg of mutton that had been stolen by a sweep, and been in the Police Office. Our 'old legs' don't get into high company when they leave our society."

For the leg Bill was supplied with the "raal Durham" in the shape of twelve months' imprisonment.

The
Pleasure-
Party

❖

No kind of literature can be more detrimental to morals than that of which we have had some melancholy examples from the London press, where the colours that belong to romance are thrown over pictures of crime otherwise revolting. Nor is much required for this kind of writing,—a touch of fate calling for sympathy, or a dash of cleverness extorting admiration, will suffice. Shave the fellow's head, and put a canvas jacket on him, and you have your hero as he ought to be. See M'Pherson with the fiddle out of his hands, and think of his beating the rump of a poor widow's cow which he had stolen, and was to feed on half raw, like a savage, as he was, and what comes of Burns' immortal song? Catch nature painting up those things with any other colours than those of blood and mud. And yet I have been a little weak sometimes in this way myself, when I have found boldness joined to dexterity. One needs an effort to get quit of rather natural feelings in contemplating some four youths, male and female, well endowed in person and intellect, and with so much of that extraneous elegance derived from the tailor and a well-practised imitation of the great, set down to plan an invasion of a foreign country, strange to them in language and manners, and with no other weapons for spoil than their boldness and their wits. A little attention enables us to disabuse ourselves, by pointing out that the boldness is impudence, and the invention deceit, and we come pleasantly back to the huckaback— the rig and furrow, and the shaved head.

In September 1856, I was in Princes Street on a general survey. It was a fine day for the time of the year, and the street was crowded with that mixed set of people, preponderating so much towards the grand and gay, for which that famous promenade has of late years become remarkable. Yes, there has been a change going on, and I have marked it:—a far more expensive style of dressing in the middle classes—a more perfect imitation of the gait and manners of the higher, so that I defy you to tell a shopkeeper's son or daughter from a lord's—more of the grandees, too, and ten foreigners for one formerly seen—the only indelible mark remaining being that of the female "unfortunates", destined to be for ever distinguished, and something about my old friends which they cannot conceal from a practised eye. Between St David Street and St Andrew Street, my attention was claimed by two ladies and a gentleman, who appeared to me to be English. They were what we call "tops",—that is, you could hardly suppose it possible for one to be more obliged to the secretion of the silk-worm, or the ingenuity of the tailor or milliner. It was far more easy for me to mark them than to give you reasons why they had an interest for me. What though I were to say that they appeared a degree too curious about the dresses of the lady-promenaders, and verified too much the common saying, which really has no reference to pocket-fanciers, that if you look in at a window, you will presently find people at your back?

At any rate, I thought I had some claims upon them, not that they were "old legs", as we call the regulars, for, as I have hinted, they were entirely new to me, but that it appeared they thought they had claims upon others,—the natural claims, you know, that are born with us. A new-born infant will hang at any breast, or even fix to a glass nipple, and these people only retain their infantine nature. So I told Riley to show deference, and keep off before them, always within eyeshot, while I kept up my interesting observation. I soon noticed that they were hopeful, with all that fidgettiness which belongs to flattering expectation. They wanted something, and would doubtless have been glad to see an old lady or gentleman faint; but there were none in that way, and no runaway horse would strike against a lamp-post, and throw its rider on the pavement. Neither did those clots of people at the windows seem worthy of their attention, yet they flitted about them, parted to meet again, and were as active as butterflies whirling in the air, and sucking no honey. With all this idle play, they kept up their cheerfulness, indulging in jokes, laughter, and other high jinks, so that I was doubtful whether they were less happy than I.

With the same fluttering levity, indulged in amidst what appeared to me might have been considered heavy expectations, they all three went tripping gaily up St Andrew Street, at the top of the northern division of which they met a very little dapper dandy, not over five feet and an inch or two. A more exquisite miniature for the cabinet of a fine lady I have never seen before,—dressed, brushed, combed, studded, ringed, and anointed; and so nimble, that if Gulliver had put him into his coat-pocket, it wouldn't have been without danger to his silver snuff-box. He seemed to be the friend of the taller belle, and, as I afterwards learned, bore the historical name of Beaumont, while she travelled by the name of Miss Mary Grant; the other, Evans, was devoted to the lesser lady, Miss Mary Smith. The little man must have been more successful than they, if I could judge from a united laugh which followed a stealthy glimpse of something which he showed cautiously, and which I naturally took for a purse. They seemed to have much in hand—one pointing one way—another, another—then a few minutes' deliberation, not without signs of impatience, as if they thought they were losing time. At length Beaumont, who, though small, seemed to be the leader, pointed north, drawing out the while a watch, and they appeared decided, all setting off along St Andrew Square. I immediately concluded they were for Scotland Street station, for I knew the northern train went about the time, and there is there often a conveniently crowded platform.

My conjecture was right. The party made direct for Scotland Street, and I signalled for Riley, who had kept his distance, without losing his vision. We followed, keeping apart, and enjoyed as we went the frolics of the party, who, coming from the heart of civilisation, probably considered themselves among some savage people, who could not help admiring—and would not be difficult to rob. As for the police of Scotland, they need not be much considered, and they at least had not heard of so humble an individual as I. So new to the town were they, that one of them, taking me by surprise, came running back, and asked me the way to the station. It was Miss Mary Grant.

"Very easy, ma'am—down to the end of the street, turn the railing on the left, and go round till you come to Scotland Street on a line with this."

"Thank you, sir, and much obliged."

Your *obligation* may be increased by and by, said I to myself, as I saw her hopping on to join the party—not the first time I've been asked the way to the net.

Miss Mary had understood my directions very well, for they never hesitated or stopped till they got to the top of the stair leading to the station-house. Being so utterly unknown to our English friends, there was no necessity for my usual caution; and accordingly, the moment they disappeared, Riley and I went forward to the parapet overlooking the stair and platform, and placing our elbows upon it, we put ourselves in the position of lounging onlookers. Our point of observation was excellent. We could see the entire platform, and everything that was going on there. A crowd of people were there, among whom a number of likely ladies, with pockets far better filled than those of mere promenaders in Princes Street. A kindred feeling might suggest to our "party of pleasure", that people can't travel now-a-days without a considerable sum of money with them, and therefore wherever there was a pocket there would also be money. And then the habit of purse-carrying, which brings all the money together—the notes in one end, and the silver or gold in the other— is a preparation just made for thieves, a convenience for which, with little time to spare, they cannot be too grateful. My friends seemed to be delighted with the bustling assemblage, but then it was to last only for a few minutes, when the train would be down, and the platform left in solitude. So they behoved to make hay while the sun shone, and they knew it. The first observation I made was to the effect that they took no tickets—just as I suspected. My second, that they began play at once, though with care, and in that shy way preliminarily to the required boldness when the hurry-scurry would begin with the coming of the train. It rather seemed that they only *marked* victims in the meantime—keeping separate—threading the crowd with alacrity and hope, picking up suitabilities by rapid glances.

Then came the rumble of the train down the tunnel, at the sound of which the passengers began to move, carrying their luggage to the edge of the platform, and all on the tiptoe of expectation. But now I fairly admit that I never more regretted so much the want of half-a-dozen of eyes. The nimble artistes were all at work at the same time—they were, in short, in a hurry of pocket-picking; and though myself cool enough, I was for an instant or two under the embarrassment of a choice to direct my vision from one to another, or to fix upon one. Miss Mary Smith was at the farther end—Evans busy helping a fat lady with her luggage—the little Beaumont deep among floating silks, and invisible. My mark was Miss Grant, who was devoted to the first-class passengers, and though versatile in the extreme, had a main chance in her eye, a lady who afterwards turned out to be Mrs C——n in Danube Street. From this lady, I saw her take a purse, just as the silk gown was being pulled in after the body. The whistle blows, away goes the train, and our friends are left all but alone on the platform.

It was now our time. Moving slowly—for though they had been in a great hurry, that was no reason for my being so too—accompanied by Riley, I entered the door at the top of the gangway, where we met the party coming up. Miss Mary Grant had not had time even to deposit her purse in her pocket, and Riley seizing her hand took it from her. They saw at once that they had been watched, and the face of the Miss Mary, whom I had directed to the scene, paled under my eye. A sign to the porters behind me brought them ready to help, and the station-master coming forward, with his assistance we bundled the whole four into the station-house. A telegraphic message was instantly sent to Burntisland, calling for the lady who had been robbed to return, and I then proceeded to search my "party of pleasure". The purse captured contained only 9s. 6d., but from their pockets altogether I took notes to the amount of £50. And next came an evidence of the strength of that friendship which exists among this class of people, and which in those four, in particular, appeared to be so strong and heartfelt only a short time before. They swore beautiful English oaths that no one of them was known to the other; and as to the unfortunate Mary, who had the purse, they all repudiated her, even the dapper Beaumont, who swore that he was an English gentleman of family, connected distantly—how far, a point of honour prevented him from condescending on—with the noble family of that name. But if the unhappy Mary was thus disowned, she could be a self-sacrifice, for she acknowledged that she did not know them, and that she had angled on her own hook. We had thus, like a bomb thrown among combustibles, severed a very close connexion; but then I had the consolation to think that we would be able to bring them together again at the bar of the court, where, if they should be once more separated, they might celebrate the occasion with tears.

It was, I admit, rather an occasion that, on which, helped by the station-master and the gallant porters, and escorted by an admiring crowd who wondered at such fine gentry being in the hands of the police, I conducted my swells to my place of deposit. I'm not sure if we had not some hurras, though I did not court notoriety of this kind; but the moment the people got an inkling they were English thieves, the old feelings between the nations seemed to rise up again—at least I could see nothing but satisfaction in the faces around us; nor was my satisfaction less when I introduced my friends to my superior, who doubtless did not expect the honour of receiving in his chambers four persons so distinguished, one being no less than a Beaumont—by Jupiter, 5 feet 2 inches, by the line!

The great Jack Cade, after swaying thousands of people, at last fell into the hands of a very simple clown. So here, as we soon understood, I had had the good fortune, in a very accidental way, of catching, at the very commencement of their Scotch career, four of the most celebrated of the English swells. They were quite well known to the authorities of London, Liverpool, and Manchester, where they had exercised their skill with so much adroitness that they had slipt through many well-drawn loops of the law; and having escaped so often there, where the detectives are supposed to be so much cleverer than ours, they had some grounds for the hope so well expressed by their hilarity, short-lived as it was, that they would again cross the borders well loaded with Scotch booty.

Next day Mrs C——n obeyed the telegraph—an instrument, by the by, which seems to have more command at the end of the wire than spoken or written words, the more by token, perhaps, that it speaks like old Jove, through lightning. She at once identified the purse with the 9s. 6d.—yes, that 9s. 6d. which condemned parties who had ravished England of hundreds, and brought down a pillar of the house of Beaumont. The trial was just as easy an affair as the capture. Sheriff Hallard, that judge so steeled against all difference between rich and poor, genteel or ungenteel, tried them. I figured more than I desired or merited in his speech—which, by the by, I would like to reproduce, but I fear to affront the honour able judge's eloquence. There is no harm in an attempt at showing my powers of memory, when I give warning that they are feeble in forensic display, whatever they may be in retaining the faces of thieves.

"Prisoners, you have been found guilty of robbing from the person. It is not often that I have to pass sentence on people of your description from England, but I hope the circumstance of my being a Scottish judge will not be held to sway me in the discharge of my duty. Yet I am not sure if the circumstance of your being English men and women is not a considerable aggravation of your crime. What did Scotland ever do to you that you should come here, hundreds of miles, to prey upon her unwary subjects? Was it not rather that you thought her honest and simple people would become easy victims in hands made expert by efforts to elude the grasp of English authorities? You forgot, too, that in comparison of England we are poor, and less able to lose what we earn by hard labour. But such considerations have small weight with persons of your description, who, if you can get money to be spent in debauchery, care little whether it come from the rich or the poor. Now the issue has proved that you had made a wrong calculation, not only as to the intelligence and sharpness of our people, but the boldness and adroitness of our detectives; and I hope you will bear in mind, and tell your compeers in England, what we fear they sometimes forget, that we have not renounced our emblem of a thistle—the pricks of which you may expect to feel, when I now sentence you to sixty days' hard labour. I am only sorry it cannot be made months,—a period more suited to your offence. For the advantage you thus gain, you are indebted to that cleverness in Mr M'Levy and his assistant by which you were so soon caught; for if you had been allowed to go on, you would have earned the attention of the High Court, and the privilege of being transported. I hope you may profit by the lesson he has taught you."

The
Tobacco-
Glutton

❖

It is almost a peculiarity of the thief that he is in his furtive appetite omnivorous. Everything that can be reduced to the chyle of money is acceptable to him. While others have predilections, he has absolutely one. It is not that he is always, however, or even often in need, and therefore glad to seize whatever comes in his way. I have known instances where he was by no means driven to his calling by necessity, and yet not only was the passion to appropriate strong in him, but he was at same time regardless of the kind of prey. Yes; it would seem as if his passion sprang out of an inverted view of property, so that the word "yours" incited him to change its meaning. As a certain valorous bird becomes ready for war the moment a brother of the same species is placed opposite to him on the barn-floor, so the regularly-trained "appropriator" gluggers and burns to be at a "possessor," as representing in his person some actual commodity. As a consequence of this strange feeling I have found, however unlikely it may appear, that thieves have really nothing of the common sense of property—that is, love to it—after they obtain it. Unless for the supply of a want, they often treat what they have stolen as if they not only did not care for it, but absolutely wished it out of their possession,—not from fear of being detected by its presence, but for some *loathing* not easily accounted for. I have a case, however, of a real predilective *artiste*, the more curious that it stands in my books almost alone.

The way in which I became acquainted with Peter Sutherland was singular enough. I was, in April 1837, walking in the Meadows, where I have more than once met wandering stagers whom I could turn to account of my knowledge of mankind. I came up to a young man very busy sending from a black pipe large clouds of tobacco smoke. Always on the alert to add to my number of profiles, I felt some curiosity about this lover of the weed, and going up to him, I made my very usual request for a light.

"By all means," said he, as he drew out his matchbox (and matches were then dear, sometime after Jones's monopoly) and struck for me what I wanted; "and I can fill your pipe too," said he, "for I like a smoker."

"Very well," said I, as I handed him my pipe, which was not out of the need of a supply; "I like a smoke, though I cannot very well tell why."

"Why, just because, like me, you like it," said he laughing; "it makes one comfortable. I deny the half of the rhyme—

> Tobacco and tobacco reek,
> It maks me weel when I'm sick;
> Tobacco and tobacco reek,
> When I'm weel it maks me sick.

It never makes me sick,——I smoke at all times, sick or well, night or day, in or out, working or idle."

"You carry it farther than I do," said I, "or, I rather think, than any body I ever knew. I cannot touch the pipe when I'm unwell."

"I never found myself in that way yet," replied he. "I believe if death could take a cutty within those grinning teeth of his, I would smoke a pipe with him."

"But it must cost you much money," said I, as I glanced at his seedy coat and squabashed hat.

"Oh, I can keep it off the price of my dinner," was the reply.

"But does it not dry your throat and make you yearn for ale?"

"Never a bit; though water, I admit, is a bad smoking drink. I take the ale when I can get it, and if you'll stand a pot, this minute I'm ready. If I can't get it, I stick to the tobacco."

"And if you can't get the tobacco," said I, with more meaning perhaps than he wotted, "what do you do?"

"That never happened yet,' replied he, with a chuckle, "and it never will."

"You wouldn't steal it would you?"—a question much in my way.

"I hope not," said he; "but if I did, 'twould only be the starved wretch taking a roll out of the baker's basket, and you know that's not punishable. My roll is just of another kind."

"You'd better not try the experiment."

"Never fear," said he; "I intend always to smoke my own twist, and have a bit to give to a friend in need."

And under the influence of this generous sentiment, he sent forth a cloud worthy of Jove's breath to send it away into thin air, and leaving me, he struck off in the direction of the links, probably to see the golfers. As I looked after him, there he was blowing away in the distance, and apparently not less happy than King Coil, albeit that king was of a nation that loved another weed. I have known great smokers, but never found that the passion, like that of opium, goes on without a term. It has a conservative way about it, I think, and cares its own excess by producing a reaction in the stomach somehow. I have noticed, too, that the greatest smokers give up at some period of their lives, almost always—at least much oftener than the moderate-cloud compellers.

But be all that as it may, it is certain that I looked upon my friend as a kind of tobacco-glutton, only a curiosity not in my way, nor did I expect that he would ever be so. I say not, being unaware that I have learned my readers a bad habit in looking for some ingenious connexion where none as yet exists—just as if I were a weaver of a cunning web, where the red thread is taken up where it suits me. By no means so, I may say; but will I thereby prevent you throwing your detective vision before my narrative, when I begin to tell you that some considerable time after this interview with my tobacco-fancier, I got information of a robbery of a grocer's shop at Ratho, from which a great many articles were taken, among the rest several rolls of tobacco, besides a number of ounces? Just the man, you will say, and so said I, as I went over the description of the thief as given to the grocer by some neighbours who saw him hanging about the shop. I recollected my friend perfectly; but in order to abate your wonder at such coincidences, please to remember that I was in the habit of going up to every lounger I met, and that I have so retentive a remembrance of faces, that I have a hundred times picked out my man from impressions derived from these casual encounters. I had never seen my tobacco-lover before nor after, and knew no more where to go for him, than where to look for another such jolly smoker out of Holland.

One night (just the old way) I was walking, with Mulholland behind me, down towards the west end of West Crosscauseway. My object at the time, I recollect, was to observe what was going on about Flinn's house in that quarter; and I frankly confess, that so little hope had I of ever seeing my old friend of the Meadow Walk, that I was thinking nothing about him; nor when I saw a lounging-like fellow—it was in the gloaming—standing at the turn of the street speaking to a woman, had I the slightest suspicion that he was one on whom I had any claims for attention; and perhaps if there is to be a miracle in the matter, by hook or crook, it consisted in this, that with a view to get a nearer look of him to see whether he belonged to Flinn's, I again went up to ask, what I did not want, a light. My first glance satisfied me that I had my tobacco-fancier before me; but I was perfectly satisfied he had no recollection of his friend of the Meadow Walk, and with this confidence I could enjoy a little fun. He took my pipe quite frankly.

"Why, there's nothing in it," said he, with the old generosity, "I will fill it for you, for I don't like to see a smoker with his pipe not only out, but empty."

And taking out a pretty large piece of tobacco, he twisted off a bit, took out a knife, and bidding me hold my hand, he cut it into shreds, filled my pipe, and lighted it.

"You seem to have plenty of tobacco," said I.

"Oh yes," said he; "and since you seem to be smoked out, I'll give you a quid for supper."

And to be sure he was not slack in giving me at least a quarter of an ounce.

"Capital stuff," said I, as I blew away; "where do you get it?"

"Special shops," said he; "I won't have your small green-shop article.

I admit to have been a little cruel in this case, for I felt an inclination to play with my old friend, and straightway gave him the end of the thread he had drawn in the Meadows. By and by he got on in the old strain in praise of the object of his passion.

"It makes me comfortable," and so forth, reverting again to the rhyme, to the half of which he again demurred, and which I really rejoiced to hear, nor can help repeating—

> Tobacco and tobacco reek,
> It maks me weel when I'm sick;
> Tobacco and tobacco reek,
> When I'm weel it maks me sick.

Restraining my laughter, and recurring again to the subject of the shop where such excellent stuff was to be got,

"In Edinburgh?" said I.

"No," said he, grandly, "there's no such thing in Edinburgh. It's made by a special manufacturer, who uses the best young leaf from Virginia, and who wouldn't put a piece of common continental stuff in—no an' it were to make his fortune. Ah, he likes a good smoke himself, and that's the reason, as I take it."

"It's so wonderfully good stuff," said I, preparing for my last whiff, "that if I knew where to send for half a pound, I would be at the expense of the carriage. I see no reason why you should keep it a secret; such a manufacturer deserves encouragement. Come, is it at Leith, where so much of the real thing is smuggled?"

"Never uses smuggled tobacco," said he, as he looked to the woman with complacent smile, as if, according to my thought, he wanted to appear big in her presence—a little simple even I myself in this thought, as you will see immediately. "I find no use," he added, "in blowing in the Queen's face."

"Ratho?" said I.

And the word was no sooner out, than the girl went off like a flash, proving thereby that she was an accomplice, and he at the same instant; and, before I could seize him, he made up the

Potterrow like a Cherokee Indian throwing away his calumet of peace in escaping from war. I made instantly after him, quickened by the conviction of my folly in uttering the charmed *word* without using at the same time my *hand*. Being supple in those days, and, though I say it, a first-rate runner, sufficient to have coped with Lapsley himself—whom I had afterwards something to do with, though not in the running line—I made up with my man in the entry leading from the Potterrow to Nicolson Square, where, collaring him, I brought him to a stand. He became quite peaceful, and as I walked him to the Office, I let him up to our old acquaintanceship—the recollection of the part he took in which, so like the conversation into which I had so playfully led him, made him bite his lip for his stupidity.

"I fear you will now know," said I, "whether your case of the starved wretch and the roll is applicable to your *roll*. I put you on your guard at the time, and you see what you have made of it."

"Tobacco !" said the poor fellow with a groan, which went to my heart like so many other groans necessitated to be shut out. "I began to smoke when a mere child. I imitated my father. The passion grew upon me by degrees, till I came to spend more money on it than I did upon meal. I was never happy unless I was steeped in the beloved lethargy, and always miserable when I could not get it. It has been to me what drink is to so many. I would have pawned my coat for a pipeful; ay, and I have pawned for it. Surely this is God's work following the devil's."

And letting his head drop upon his breast, he groaned again deeper than before.

"Yes," said I, "you have been upon the sliding scale. You began with a *whiff*; and you will end with a *blast* that will carry you to Botany Bay."

"Yes, yes," he responded₁ "I now see that a very small gratification may be fed up into a passion, and that passion to a crime, and then the burst." And after some time he added, "But maybe the judges may have pity on me; when they know how I was pushed on from less to more."

"Then they would pity all that come before them," said I; "all crimes have small beginnings and big endings."

And so I took him to the Office, where I proceeded to search him, and here is something curious: He wore a kind of bonnet—a Gilmerton bonnet, because it is usually worn by the carters of that village. The article has often a hoop in it, to keep it light on the head; and concealed in the case of the hoop there were a number of plies of the stolen twist. Nor was this all. On pulling up the legs of his trousers, there were discovered three or four ply on each leg, serving the purpose of garters. Then within his neckcloth there were so many plies, that he might have been said to have had a tobacco neckerchief. You might have called him a tobacco idol, fitted for being set up to be worshipped by the votaries of the leaf.

No doubt he admitted afterwards that he had stolen from the shop the other articles amissing, but he asserted that it was the desire to possess the tobacco that urged him to the robbery, and that once being in he had laid hold of whatever came to his hand. I cannot help remarking, that my poor tobacco-fancier paid dear for his quid, in giving for it seven long years of servitude in Botany Bay. I have sometimes wondered whether, when there, he ever took a pipe into his mouth. Not unlikely.

The
Whiskers

❖

It may be naturally supposed that we detectives are not much given to sadness. It is, I suspect, a weakness connected with me, a tendency to meditate on the vanity of human wishes; and I should be free from the frailty, insomuch as there has been less vanity in my wishes to apprehend rogues than in the case of most other of the artistes of my order. Yet am I not altogether free from the weakness. We have a natural wish to see our friends happy around us, and this desire is the source of my little frailty; for when I find my ingenious friends off my beat, and away elsewhere, I immediately conclude they are being happy at the expense of others, and I am not there to sympathise; nor does it affect this tendency much that I am perfectly aware that my sympathy rather destroys their happiness.

I had, about April 1854, lost sight for a time of the well known Dan Gillies. He had had my sympathies more than once, and immediately took to melancholy; but somehow or another he recovered his gaiety,—a sure enough sign that he again stood in need of my condolence. I had been told that in kindness he and his true-hearted Bess M'Diarmid had gone to the grazing on turnips, (watches,) and that I had small chance of seeing him for a time. Well, here was an occasion for a return of my fit, for wasn't Dan happy somewhere, and I not there to see. I don't say I was thinking in that particular direction on that 5th day of April when I was walking along Princes Street, for indeed I was looking for another natural-born gentleman among those who, considering they have better claims to promenade that famous street, pretend to despise those who, I have said, are nearer to natural rights than they are; but indulging in that habit of side-looking, which I fear I have borrowed from my friends, who persist in an effort to avoid a straight, honest look at me, I descried a well-known face under a fine glossy silk hat, and above a black and white dappled cravat. A glance satisfied me that the rest of the dress was in such excellent harmony that he might, two minutes before, have come out of the Club, where plush and hair-powder stands at the door. It was Dan. The grazing must have been rich to give him so smooth and velvety a coat; and to show that he had not despised his fare, he had a yellow "shaw" stretching between the middle of his fine vest to the pocket. When a grand personage, who despises the toil which makes us all brethren, meets one of my humble, laborious order, he makes a swerve to a side, even though the wind is in another direction, to avoid the blasting infection of common humanity, and Dan was here true to his class; but as I do not discard the duties any more than the rights of nature, I overlooked the insult, and swerved in the same direction, not being confident enough, nevertheless, to infect with my touch the hand of a Blue-Vein, if not a Honeycomb.

"Why, Dan," said I, as I faced him, and somewhat interrupted his passage, "what a fine pair of whiskers you've got since I saw you. The turnips must have been reared on the real Peruvian."

"What the d——l have you to do with my whiskers?"

"One who has been the means of shaving your head," replied I, "may surely make amends by rejoicing in the growth of your fine hair elsewhere."

"None of your gibes. Be off. I owe no man anything."

"No, Dan, but every man, you know, owes you, if you can make him pay. Don't you know what's up?"

"No, and don't care."

"There's a grand ship-launch at Leith to-day."

"D——n your ship-launch!" said the Honeycomb; and pushing me aside, Dan strutted away under the indignation of the shame of my presence.

I could not help looking after him, and recollecting the remark of Lord Chesterfield on the South-Sea Islander who sat at table in the company of lords. Looking at his back you could perceive no difference between him and a high-bred aristocrat. But the aristocrats don't mind those thin distinctions.

Having some much more important business in hand that day, all recollection of Dan and his whiskers passed out of my mind. I remember I had to meet a French lackey who could point out to me a London brewer's clerk committed to my care. The offender had run away from his employer taking with him not only the flesh which had got so lusty upon the stout, but also a couple of thousand pounds which he ought to have deposited in a bank; nor was this even the entire amount of his depredations, for he had also contrived to abstract the brewer's wife, described by my Frenchman as a "great succulent maman of forty years", and not far from that number of stones avoirdupois. With such game in prospect, it was not likely I should trouble myself with Dan Gillies, nor did I care more for the Leith launch. The constables there could look to that, though I was not the less aware that if Dan got among the crowd there would be pockets rendered lighter, without more of a "purchase" than might be applied by a thief's fingers.

Notwithstanding of the brightness of my prospects in the morning—for I had even pictured to myself the English clerk with the "succulent maman" hanging on his arm, and together promenading Princes Street—my hopes died away as the day advanced. I had got, moreover, weary of the clatter of the lackey, and was, in short, knocked up. It might be about four o'clock, I think, when I resolved upon returning by the way of the Office, where I had some report to make before going home to dinner. I proceeded slowly along Waverley Bridge, turned past the corner of Princes Street gardens, and advanced by the back of the Bank of Scotland. I was in reality at the time looking for none of my friends. I had had enough of looking and felt inclined rather to give my eyes a rest by directing them to the ground, after the manner of melancholy musers. As I was thus listlessly making my way, I was roused by a rapid step, and I had scarcely time to look up when I encountered my young Honeycomb of the morning. I was at first confused, and no great wonder, for there was Dan Gillies without a single hair upon his face. The moment he saw me he wanted to bolt, but the apparition prompted me on the instant to cross him, and hold him for a moment at bay.

"Dan, Dan," said I, with really as much unfeigned surprise as humour, "what has become of your whiskers, man?"

A fiery eye, and the terrible answer which sends a man to that place where one might suppose that eye had been lighted, so full of fury was it.

"Why, it's only a fair question," said I, again keeping my temper. "I might even wish to know the man who could do so clean a thing."

"What have you to do with my barber?"

"Why, now you are getting reasonable," said I; "your question is easily answered; I might want him, say on a Sunday morning, to do to me what he has done to you."

Again dispatched to the place of four letters with an oath which must have been forged there by some writhing soul, I could stay him no longer, for making a rush past me, Dan Gillies was off in the direction of the Fleshmarket Close, up which I saw him turn.

His oaths still rung in my ear. I have often thought of the wonderful aptitude of the grown-up Raggediers at swearing; they begin early, if they do not lisp, in defiances of God, and you will hear the oaths ringing amidst the clink of their halfpennies as they play pitch-and-toss. Their little manhood is scarcely clothed in buckram, when they would look upon themselves as simpletons if they do not vindicate their independence by daring both man and Heaven. You may say they don't understand the terms they use. Perhaps few swearers do; but in these urchins the oaths are the sparks of the steel of their souls, and there is not one of them unprepared to show by their cruelty that their terrible words are true feelings. It may appear whimsical in me, but I have often thought that if this firmness of character—for it is really a mental constitution—were directed and trained by education and religion in the track of duty, it would develop itself as an energy fitted for great and good things. A man like me has no voice in the Privy Council; but *literature*, as I have heard said, is a big whispering-gallery, whereby the humblest of minds may communicate with the highest. Let it be that my whisper is laughed at, as everything is grinned at or laughed at which is said for the hopefulness of our wynd reprobates; but I have learned by experience, that while the greatest vices spring from the dregs of society, the Conglomerates, as they are called in that book (which describes them so well,) "The Castes of Edinburgh", so the greatest virtues sometimes spring from the same source. How much of the vice they are *forced* to retain, and how much of the virtue they are compelled to lose, is one of the whispers which ought to reach the ears of the great.

At the time Dan left me, I was not in this grand way of thinking. Nay, to be very plain, I was laughing in my sleeve; because, in the first place, a detective is not a Methodist preacher; and in the second place, because I have a right to my fun as well as others; and in the third place, because I came to the conclusion that Dan Gillies had some reason for shaving his whiskers which ought to interest me. In short, I had no doubt that Dan and his "wife" had been at the ship-launch.

With the laugh, I suppose, still hanging about my lips as a comfortable solace after my ineffectual hunt after the brewer's clerk and the jolly maman, I entered the Office, where the first information I got was, that a lady had been robbed of her purse at Leith, and that a young wench was in hands there as having been an accomplice along with a swell of a pickpocket who had escaped.

"I was thinking as much," said I, with a revival of my laugh; "I know the man."

And so I might well say, for I had now got to the secret of the shaved whiskers.

"What mean you?" said the Lieutenant.

"Why, just that if you want the man, I will bring him to you. I will give you the reason of my confidence at another time."

"To be sure we want him," was the rather sharp reply of my superior.

"Then I will fetch him," said I.

And so I went direct to Brown's Close, where I knew the co-partnership of Gillies and M'Diarmid formerly carried on business, both in the domestic and trading way. Domestic! what a strange word as applied to these creatures—charm, as it is, to conjure up almost all the associations which are contained in the whole round of human happiness! Yes, I say domestic; happiness is a thing of accommodation. These beings will go forth in the morning in the spring of hope, and after threading dangers which are nothing less than wonderful, jinking the throw of the loop of the line which grazes their very shoulders, and turning and doubling in a thousand directions to escape justice, they meet at nightfall to *enjoy* the happiness of a home. The beefsteak, as it fries, gives out the ordinary sound, the plunk of the drawn cork is heard, and they narrate their hairbreadth escapes, their dangers, and their triumphs. They laugh, they sleep, but their enjoyment terminates with my knock at the door. The solitary inmate is wondering at the absence of the female without whom the word "domestic" becomes something like a mockery. It is needless to deny him affections; he has them, and she has them, as the tiger and the tigress have them. They don't complain like other folk, because they don't bark or growl at Providence; but the iron screw is in the heart. I have read its pangs in the very repression of its expression.

I had been so quick in my movements that I went right in upon my man just as he had entered, no doubt after the cautious doublings consequent upon our prior interview. The salutation given me was a growl of the wrath which had been seething in the Pappin's digestor of his heart.

"What right have you to hound me in this way?" he cried, as he closed his fist and then ground his teeth.

"Why, Dan," said I, calmly, "I'm still curious about the whiskers."

"Whiskers again," he roared.

"Aye, just the whiskers," said I. "I have told you I am curious about them, and I want to know why you parted with what you seemed so proud of?"

"Gibe on; you'll make nothing of me," he cried again. "I defy you."

"Well, but I cannot give up the whiskers in that easy way," said I, "because I have an impression that if the lady in Leith had not lost her purse, your whiskers would still have clothed your cheeks."

From which cheeks the colour fled in an instant. Even to the hardest of criminals the pinch of a fact is like the effect of a screw turned upon the heart. It is only we who can observe the changes of their expression. Dan knew, in short, that he was caught; and I have before remarked that the regular thieves can go through the business of a detection in a regular way.

"Well," he said, as he felt the closing noose, and with even a kind of grim smile, "I might as well have kept my hair."

"Never mind," said I, "it will have time to grow in the jail. Come along. The cuffs?"

"Oh no, I think you have no occasion. Them things are only for the irregulars, you know. But do you think you'll mend Daniel Gillies by the jail?"

"No," said I, "I don't expect it."

"Then why do you intend to send me there?"

"Why," replied I, in something like sympathy for one who I knew to be of those who are trained to vice before they have the choice of good or evil laid before them, "just because it is my trade."

And, strange as it may seem, I observed a tear start into his red eye.

"Your trade," said he, as he rubbed the cuff of his coat over his face, "your trade; and have you a better right to follow it than I have to pursue mine? You didn't learn yours from your father and mother, did you?"

"No, Dan, but I know you did."

"Yes, and the more's the pity," replied he, as he got even to an hysterical blubber. "I have had thoughts on the subject. Even when last in the Calton I could not sleep. Something inside told me I was wronged, but not by God—by man. I was trained by fiends who made money by what they taught me, and I have been pursued by fiends all my life. When was a good lesson ever given me, or a kindly word ever said to me, except by a preacher in the jail with a Bible in his hand? Suppose I had listened to him, and when I got out had taken that book into my hand, and had gone to the High Street and bawled out, 'Put me to a trade, employ me, and give me wages.' Who would have listened to me? A few pence from one, and the word 'hypocrite' from another, and then left to my old shifts, or starve. Take me up, but you'll never mend me by punishment."

I always knew Dan to be a clever fellow, but I was not prepared for this burst. Yet I knew in my heart it was true.

"Well," said I, "Dan, I pity you. I have often thought that if that old villain David, and that old Jezebel Meg, who were your parents, had not corrupted you, you had heart and sense to be a good boy."

"Ay, and it has often wrung my heart," he replied, "when I have seen others who were born near me, though only in Blackfriars' Wynd, respectable and happy, and I a criminal in misery by the chance of birth; but all this is of no use now. Then where's Bess, poor wretch?"

"She's in Leith jail."

"Right," cried he, as he blubbered again. "I sent her there. She was a playmate of mine, and I led her on in the path into which I was led. She might have been as good as the best of them."

And the poor fellow, throwing himself on a chair, cried bitterly.

I have encountered more than one of these scenes. They have only pained me, and seldom been of any service to the victims themselves. Were a thousand such cases sent up to the Privy Council, I doubt if their obduracy in endowing ragged and industrial schools would be in the slightest degree modified.

I believe little more passed. I had my duty to perform, and Dan was not disobedient. That same evening he was sent to Leith. He was afterwards tried. He was identified by the lady and a boy who knew him, and sentenced to twelve months. Bess got off on the plea of not proven. I lost all trace of them, but have no hopes that either the one or the other was mended by the detection through the whiskers. The hair would grow again not more naturally than would spring up the old roots of evil planted by those who should have engrafted better shoots on the stock of nature.

The
Club
Newspaper

❖

The sliding scale is so far applicable to us as well as to thieves. As the latter proceed from crime to crime, the less to the greater—in the scarlet tint from the lighter to the deeper, so we slide on from trace to trace till we get to the fountain. And there is this similarity, too, between the cases. Our beginnings are small, but they are hopeful, and as the traces increase, we get more energetic and bolder: so with the thieves; there is an achieved success which leads to the greater triumph. Nay, I have known the parallel carried further. If we fail in one attempt, we try again; and I have a case to give, but not just now, where the urchin Gibbon's first attempt at a till, from which he appropriated *one farthing*, and for which he was punished by confinement, was quickly succeeded by a greater triumph, to the amount of *seventeen shillings and sixpence*. My present case has a peculiarity, in so far as I contrived to make a *paltry* theft the lever whereby to raise up another of a serious description.

In 1840, Mr Ellis, the manager of the Queen Street Club, was exposed to much trouble, suspicion, and difficulty, by complaint after complaint, on the part of the officers frequenting and sleeping in the house, that money, in five and ten-pound notes, had been taken from their portmanteaus. The case was painful to Mr Ellis in more respects than one; for although no suspicion could attach to him, yet in all such concealed robberies, the natural shades that spread everywhere over all in positions liable to be suspected, require to be elevated or dispersed by the light of reason, and that light comes always with an effort. Mr Ellis came to the Office, and I got my charge. I saw at once that the culprit was one of the waiters;

but then there were several in the house, and I knew all the difficulties of a case of that kind. The wider spread the suspicion, the
less easy the concentration. I would do my best, and Mr Ellis had
confidence at least in my zeal.

Repairing, accordingly, to the Club one forenoon, I questioned
Mr Ellis as to the habits of the waiters, and, in particular, which of
them lived out of the house. I found that one man, Donald M'Leod,
had a house in Rose Street, with a wife and no children; and in
order that I may not take too much credit to myself, I may state that
that man was more suspected by his master than any of the others.
I was now so far on my way. I called the waiters together in a room
with closed doors.

"Now, gentlemen," (that's my polite way) "I have to inform you
that there is a robber among you. Bags and portmanteaus have for a
lengthened period been opened in this house, and sums of money
extracted. All who are innocent will be glad to answer in the
affirmative to my question. Will you consent to your trunks and
persons being searched?"

"Yes," answered every one.

"Donald M'Leod," continued I, "an honest married man, with a
decent wife, I have no doubt can have no objection to my going to
his house and taking a look about it—not that I have any suspicion
of him because he lives out of the Club, but that his trunks being at
home, I must make him like the others."

"No objection," replied honest Donald, whose honesty, however, did not sit so easy upon him as honest Rab's of certain romantic notoriety.

"You will all remain here till I finish my process in the house."

To which last question having got the answer I expected, I went
out and told Mr Ellis to take care that no messenger should, in the
meantime, be allowed to leave the house. The search among the
trunks yielded me just as much as I expected—perhaps a little
more, in the shape of certain love epistles, which might have made
a little fortune to the street speech-criers. What a strange under-
current, swirling in eddies, does love keep for ever moving! But

what had I to do with love, who only wanted money,—two things that are so often cruelly separated, but which should be for ever joined.

I then proceeded to Rose Street, and soon finding my house, I knocked gently. A quiet, decent-looking woman opened it.

"Are you Mrs M'Leod?"

"Ay," she answered without fear or suspicion, for what did she know of James M'Levy the thief-catcher?

"Well, my good woman," said I, as I shut the door behind me somewhat carefully, and afterwards sat down, "you don't know, I fancy, that some things have been amissing belonging to the gentlemen of the Club? Donald, no doubt, so far as I know, is innocent; but as all the waiters, like honest men, have consented that their trunks should be searched, it is but fair, you know, that I should take a look through your house, to put them all on a footing of equality."

"And that's right," said she, with really so little timidity, or rather with so much apparent sincerity, that, if I had not been M'Levy, I would have thought that Donald was an honest man after all.

With this permission, and under so kindly a sanction, I commenced my search, by no means a superficial one—perhaps deeper in proportion to Mrs M'Leod's seeming sincerity. It was not altogether unsuccessful—small thefts lead on in the scale to big ones, and superficial traces to deeper. I got some newspapers, one with the Club's address, and putting them together, said—

"Mrs M'Leod, you will allow me to take these papers; I fancy Mr Ellis allows Donald, as a favourite, to take away an old one now and then to amuse him at home, and, perhaps, to read to you."

"Nae doot," said she, "ye dinna fancy Donald wad steal them."

"By no means. I never said it," replied I. I was not bound to say I never *thought* it——a little beyond my candour.

So I bade Mrs M'Leod good day, and making my way to the Club, I told Mr Ellis the result of my search.

"Well," replied he, "you have got something, and you have got nothing."

"Had Donald M'Leod any authority from you to take these papers, and this one especially directed to the Club?"

"Certainly not; but the matter is so small, that I can't see how anything can be made of it."

"And you would give up the charge ?"

"Yes; it cannot lead to my money."

"Well," said I, "if that is your decision, I bow to it; but I tell you this, that out of that solitary old newspaper I will get your money. Will you give me my own way?"

"Well, I have heard so much of your success in desperate cases, I don't care though I do."

"Agreed," said I.

And without further parley, I went to Donald, who was at the time in the lobby.

"Donald," said I, "I want you up to the Office."

"Me," replied Donald, with an ounce less blood in his cheek-veins than he had a minute before, "do you think I'm the robber?"

"I don't say so," said I; "but I want some information from you which I cannot so well get here."

And Donald, a little reconciled, and with a little of the blood in the act of returning, took his hat.

When I got him to the Office, I immediately clapped him into a cell, and locking the door, was under way once more for Rose Street.

"Mrs M'Leod," said I, as the honest Gael opened the door, and shut it, "I am a little vexed."

"What's the matter? I hope naething's wrang wi' Donald?"

"Why, not much," said I; "I am only troubled about these old useless newspapers. The authorities up the way—dangerous creatures these authorities—have taken it into their wise heads that Donald stole the papers from the Club; nay, they have locked him up in a cell as dark as pitch, with bread and water for fare, and, I fear, no hope of anything but judgment and punishment."

"Fearfu' news!" said the woman. "Oh, terrible news! condemn a man for an auld newspaper!" and hiding her face in her hands, she burst into tears.

I need not say I pitied her, for in reality I did; for at that time I had not the slightest reason to suppose that she could know that the papers were not given to Donald, or allowed to be taken as having served their purpose, and being consequently useless.

"But there's hope," said I.

"Hope!" she cried, "Hope!" as she took away her hands, "Whaur?—how?—speak, for God's sake!"

"The charge is a small one," said I, "and I have no doubt it would be scored off, provided the missing money were got. I'm sure you don't have it; I have searched the house; but perhaps"—

"What?" she broke in, "what?"

"Perhaps you may know through Donald where it is?"

I watched her face, which was now pale. She began to think, and she did think; for if ever thought came out of a face, it might have been read in the point of her nose, sharpened by the collapse of the muscles through fear.

If in this agony she sat a minute, she sat fully five; but I was patient. I turned my face from her, and looked at nothing, perhaps because my mind was directed to something. She was under a struggle; I heard the signs,—the quick breath, the heaving chest, the sobs, the efforts to suppress them,—still I was patient and pitiful. Sad duties ours! Yes, we must steel ourselves against human woes; nay, we must turn nature's yearnings to the advantage of official selfishness. At length,

"Are you sure the newspapers will be scored aff?"

"Sure."

And then another sinking into the battle of her thoughts,—the lips quivering, the desultory movements of the hands, the jerking from one position to the other,—at length calmness—the calmness of one whose agony is over,—a rest of many minutes.

"And you're sure," she said again, as she fixed her eyes upon me, with such speech in them that my soul revolted at its very wickedness. Must I admit it? Yes, it is put upon us. A lie is one thing, the keeping deep down in our hearts the truth another. The one I abhor, the other is a duty. I knew that the money, if produced, would form a charge in place of the newspapers. I knew *she* didn't think this; but I knew also I was not bound to tell her that she was wrong in not thinking it. Nay, there are worse cases than mine, that may be and are justified every day. When robbers are at the window, and you cry, "Bring me the gun," when there is no gun in the house, you lie; but you are not bound to tell men whose hands are at your throat that you lie. There are necessities that go beyond all moral codes, and laugh at them. If this woman knew where that stolen money was, she was, by her own doing, under the sharp consequences of that necessity, and must abide the result as an atonement for an act not perpetrated under that necessity. Behold my logic! I am at the mercy of the public.

These were not my thoughts at the time; my conduct; was merely the effect of them, and I was simply watchful. At length Mrs M'Leod rose from the chair,—she stood for a moment firm,—she then went into a closet, where, having remained a little, she came forth, to my astonishment, changed; she was dressed—shawl, bonnet, and veil.

"Come with me," she said in a low voice, sorrowful, but without a tremor.

I said nothing, only obeyed. She shut the door, and proceeding down the stair, beckoned me to follow her. Not a word was spoken. We got down to the foot of the stair, then to the street, and I followed her as she led. We proceeded in this silent way until we came to Frederick Street. We then went along that street till she came to the area gate of a gentleman's house; that gate she opened, and going down the stair, she again beckoned me to follow her. We now stood before the kitchen-door, at which she rapped. The knock was obeyed, and a young woman made her appearance.

"Peggy," said Mrs M'Leod in a whisper, which I heard very well, "I ha'e come for yon."

"Yon!" muttered I to myself; strange Scotch word—something like the mysterious "it," when applied to a ghost.

"Weel!" replied the girl, "come in."

We both entered, and were led along a dark passage till we came to a bedroom—no doubt that of the young woman. We entered it, and the servant, who seemed to be struck with the sympathy of our silence, proceeded to open a blue trunk, from which she took out a small bundle, composed of a roll of a red handkerchief.

"There it is," said she, as she put it into the hands of Mrs M'Leod.

We then left the room, returning again to the kitchen, from which we proceeded into the area.

"There's the siller," said she, as she put the bundle into my hands.

I took the parcel and placed it in my pocket. We mounted the stair, and Mrs M'Leod left me. It is needless to say that I could not restrain my curiosity; nor did I try. I went down towards Princes Street Gardens, and seating myself on the parapet, proceeded to undo the red handkerchief. I found within a large bundle of bank notes, composed of tens and fives, and upon counting them found the amount to be £180. Now I fairly admit I was not satisfied. I wanted something more; and tying up my bundle I repaired again to Rose Street.

"Mrs M'Leod," said I, as I entered, "it will be necessary that you mark these notes for me. My masters, the authorities, will not believe I got them from you unless I get your name to them. Have you pen and ink ?"

"Ay," said she, "but I daurna mark them, Donald would be angry."

"But you forget the authorities," said I.

"The authorities!" she repeated, with a kind of a tremble at the very sound of the word.

"Yes, they may be angry, and you know the anger of the authorities is very different from that of Donald M'Leod."

"Very true," replied she.

And bringing the pen and ink I got her name to every note. I was *now* satisfied, and taking the direction of Queen Street, arrived at the Club, where I saw Mr Ellis.

"How much money was taken altogether?" inquired I.

"Why," said he, "I collected the different complaints, and adding up the sums found they amounted to £180."

"The Highlanders are a very careful people," said I. "The sum I have recovered, and which is tied up in this handkerchief, is just £180."

"Recovered!" said he, in astonishment. "Why, I thought it was a forlorn hope. Where in all the earth did you get it; or rather, I should ask, how?"

"Just by means of the old newspaper with the name of the Club upon it. I think I told you that if I took my own way, and not yours, I would get the cash."

"You did," replied he; "but to be very candid with you, I had no hope, though I admitted I had faith in your name. But tell me where you got it, for I am dying to know?"

"I can hardly explain all in the meantime," said I. "I am bent for the Office, and up for time. But I may inform you that Donald M'Leod is the man, and we must keep him in custody."

"The newspaper!" again ejaculated Mr Ellis, as if he was in great perplexity. "How a piece of printed paper should be the means of getting £180! Was the money marked upon it?"

"No; yet I repeat it was the means of getting your money. Of course I cannot leave the notes with you. You will get them after Donald receives his sentence."

And with this I went away, leaving Mr Ellis to divine how the old newspaper came to have so much virtue. I then proceeded to the Office, where, having deposited the money, and explained the affair to the Superintendent, I was asked, "Where is the woman?"

And I knew that this question would be asked of me, and I knew also what would be my answer.

"Why, sir," said I, "do you really think that I should be the man to apprehend that woman?"

"Strictly, you should," said he, with a smile; "but if ever there was a case in which an officer might be passed over for a duty, it is this. I would rather go for her myself than put this duty on you. I acknowledge you were justified in the words you used, that the newspapers would be scored, and that you were entitled to your mental reservation. The question may be said to be a subtle one, suited to the logic of casuists, but I affirm that it may be resolved by a sturdy moralist. As for the rest, you have shown a feeling creditable to the heart of a right man, in leaving the apprehension of the woman to another."

Mrs M'Leod was in the evening brought up by my assistant. The two were tried at the High Court, and Donald was sentenced to seven years' transportation, while Mrs M'Leod, as being under the iron rule ot the Gael, was acquitted.

The
Laugh

❖

I believe I have said, that the devil, if well examined, would be found to have a limp; and perhaps, this notion of mine may aptly enough be termed a detection, seeing I have had so many opportunities of getting near to him in those places where he rests himself in his long journeys from his principal dominions. Nor am I less satisfied that Chance is one of his female angels, who having been slighted by him, "peaches", and tells the like of me his infirmity. Surely I cannot be blamed for an opinion, however absurd it may appear to those slow-pacing people who go so little to a side, where the real curiosities of human nature lie, when I have such a case to report as the robbery of Mr Blyth's shop in the High Street, a little above the Fleshmarket Close, by M'Quarry, and a friend of that accomplished shoplifter.

One morning, a good number of years ago,—1847, I think,—I was going from my house in the Canongate to my duties in the office, at my usual hour of eight in the morning. I had not much on my mind on that occasion. No charges were then on the books, and I was beginning to think I was gaining ground against the workers of iniquity. Perhaps my mind was perfectly vacant; no one of my images being called upon to stir in their quiet resting-place in my head, and show the likenesses to their originals. In this negative state of mind, whom should I see coming up but a well-known personage of the name of M'Quarry, with whom, though so well known to me, I wished much to be even more intimate, probably with the selfish view of knowing some of his secret adventures?

It was quite natural I should fix my eye on him before he saw me, because, while I has nothing else to do, he was bent upon something.

As I wish to mix a little instruction with the benefit derived from the mere lesson I teach of the insecurity of criminals, allow me to go aside with you for a moment to a close-end,—always my school-room,—and tell you that there is a great deal more in faces than is generally supposed. All men and women pretend, less or more, to the subject, but really their study is generally limited to the inquiry whether one is pleased or displeased with you when in talk. How few ever aspire to read people as they run, to guess what they are bent upon, and how things are going with them; and yet, what a field is open to the student of human nature here! I exclude the perambulators and loungers, of course, who are always simply engaged in being looked at. Their faces are set in a fix, and you can find nothing there but a steady waiting for admiration; but in the business people, and those not above domestic troubles, you can always find something readable. I keep to my own peculiar race, and I say I am seldom *out* when I get my eyes on them. I can, for instance, always tell an unlucky thief from a lucky one,—one with "speculation in his eye" from one without a job in contemplation,— one with full fobs from one with empty pockets,—one who suspects being scented from one who is on the scent. And therefore I derive a kind of benefit; for, just as I observe a great and sudden amount of cheerfulness in the eye of a celebrity, so do I become cheerful, and a dull dog infects me like sympathy. The reason is plain enough; their cheerfulness is that cause of the cheerfulness which is in me, insomuch as it inspires me with the wish to know the particular transaction which makes them happy and so many others sad, while their sadness implies that I have nothing to discover.

On that morning, when M'Quarry came down the High Street, he was so cheerful that, as I have said, he did not see me. "Luck makes people lightly their best friends," and so he lightlied me— the very thing that fixed my gaze on him. There was something more than the mere blythesomeness in the usual clod face, which was sure proof that he had made some other unhappy—perhaps even Mr Blyth, whose shop he passed in a kind of half run, darting his eye inside with a kind of humorous triumph,—and continuing the same excited pace, he passed me. His copartner, whose name I don't recollect, but who was quite familiar to me, was behind him some few yards. He went at the same pace, had the same look of merriment, threw the same darting look into the shop, passed on, and overtook his friend. Though not quite polite to look back upon your friends, I could not resist the impulse, and I just looked in time to see them burst out in a pretty joyous laugh together, and away they went arm-in-arm.

A very simple affair. There was nothing wrong with Mr Blyth's shop, so far as I could see; and after all, what was there in a look into a shop to interest me? It might have been different at night, when a lounger is reconnoitring for the purposes of a bolt in and a bolt out; but, independently of its being the morning, the young men were off with merely a laugh on their cheek. Yes, but I was satisfied of one thing, and that was, that some game of *draughts* had been played in that shop the previous night. "Ah!" thought I, "the little fishes, when too happy with the light of the sun on the top of the waters, get tipsy, and then topsy-turvy, and turning up their white bellies so as to be seen by the gulls, get both picked up and gobbled up."

With these thought I proceeded up the High Street, and entered the office. The Captain was already there, with a gentleman standing by him—no other then Mr Blyth, whose shop had so occupied my attention in my walk.

"Oh, M'Levy, you're just in time," said the Captain. "Here is Mr Blyth with information that his shop has been broken into last night from behind, and a great quantity of silks carried off.

"It is just a case for you, M'Levy," said Mr Blyth, who gave me no time to speak; "for I fear that it is almost a desperate one. I mean we have no means of tracing, except through the goods. No one in the neighbourhood saw the burglars.'

"It is a mere case of a search for the articles," continued the Captain. "M'Levy, you can take charge. Call up some of the best searchers, and distribute them in the course of the day among the brokers. But we can expect nothing for a day or two—until the robbers begin to 'give out'."

"There's no occasion for calling in any of the men," said I; "neither is there any occasion for troubling the brokers. I know who the robbers are, and will have them up in a couple of hours. Nay, if you wait, I will bring them to you."

"What," cried the astonished silk-mercer, "already! You're surely joking. Have you been up all night?"

"No; in bed all night, sleeping as sound as a bat in winter."

"Then some policeman has been on the look-out, and told you."

"I have not spoken to a policeman today yet."

"Then how, in the name of wonder, have you got it?"

"Just through the means of a laugh," I replied, laughing myself.

"Why, you are making a joke of my loss of a hundred guineas."

"A laugh is not quite so useless a thing as you imagine. The cackle of a goose saved a city on one occasion, and the cackle of these men, who are not geese, will save your silk-mercery. I tell you I will have the burglars with you, ay, in one hour, and with them your goods. Wait till I come."

"Well, no doubt you're famous in your way, but I fear it won't do to apprehend a man for a laugh."

"I've done it for a *breath*," said I, "merely because it told me there was some fear in the breather of his breath being interrupted by a certain kind of handkerchief which you don't deal in. Sit down, and keep yourself easy."

I accordingly set to my task, going direct to M'Quarry's mother, in Hume's Close; my assistant, as usual, with me. I opened the door, and went in just as his mother was giving him his breakfast.

"You didn't notice me this morning, M'Quarry, when you passed me at Mr Blyth's door?" said I.

The word Blyth struck him to the heart.

"Blyth, wha is Mr Blyth?" said the mother, as she looked into her son's pale face, her own being nearly of the same colour.

"Why, bless you, don't you know the man you bought these silks of, up in that bole there?" pointing to the likeliest place, at the same moment that I observed something like a fringe hanging out from the crevice made by the shrunk door.

"There's nae silk there," said the mother.

"All a d—d lie," growled the son.

"There's no use for any words about that," said I, placing a chair and mounting.

On opening the door of the old cupboard, sunk in the wall, there were Mr Blyth's scarfs, neckcloths, and ribbons, all stuffed in except that bit of fringe, which had claimed my eye, and convinced me more and more that the devil has a halt; but at that very moment the door of the room burst open, overturning the chair on which I stood, and laying me sprawling on my back, confounded, but still able enough to hear the words of the intruder.

"Run, M'Quarry, M'Levy's in the close!"

"Yes, and here," I cried, starting up and seizing the speaker, just as he got alarmed; no other but my friend whose laugh, along with M'Quarry's, so delighted me in the morning.

"The laugh's on the other side now," said I.

The fellow struggled, but he was only a sapling; and as M'Quarry saw there were two to one, he started upon his feet and laid hold of me by the throat. I instantly changed hands, seizing the younger and weaker with my left, and, using the other against M'Quarry, pulled away his right, at the same time getting hold of his neckcloth, which I pulled so tight that he instantly became red in the face. I was afraid of the mother, who still held the knife in her hand with which she had been cutting the bread for her son's breakfast; but the sight of her choking son produced such an effect upon her that she set up a scream sufficient to reach the head of the close. The sound had been heard by Mulholland, who, hastening up, relieved me of one of my opponents.

"We give in," said M'Quarry, as he gasped for breath.

"That's sensible" said i. "Then you walk up with me you know where; on with your bonnet. As for you, Mrs M'Quarry, I have to ask you to accompany us; not, perhaps, that I will trouble you much, as the silks may have been placed there without your knowledge; but as I need the room for half-an-hour, and must be sure of your not entering it when I am away, you go with us, and I lock the door."

They all came very quietly. I locked the door and took the key with me, and in a few minutes had them all lodged, without communicating my capture yet to Mr Blyth, who, I understood, was still waiting. I would go by and by, however, and taking two men I hastened and got up the silks.

"Now, Mr Blyth, here are your silks and the robbers," said I, as the prisoners were brought and the mercery. "It is not two hours yet, and as this affair began with a laugh I wish it to terminate with one."

A wish complied with on the instant by every one except the culprits.

My story is ended, but there is a postscript. Mr Blyth could not, after he went away, understand my allusion to the laugh, and one day, as I was passing, he called me in, with a view to an explanation. That I gave him, much in the same way as I have given it to the reader. After considering a little, he said,—

"Well, how simple this affair is after all. It was not so much your cleverness, M'Levy, as their folly, that got me my goods.

"You never said a truer thing in your life, sir; " said I, "for people give M'Levy great praise for extraordinary powers. It is all nonsense. I am just in the position of the candid juggler, who tells his audience that there is no mystery at all in his art, when all is explained. My detections have been and are simple pieces of business,—far more simple than the schemes that end in non-detections,—and yet these have all the intricacy of some engines, which look fine on paper, but the very complexity of which prevents them from grinding your meal."